A Ghost Hunter's Guide to the

Most Haunted Houses

in America

Terrance Zepke

WHAT REVIEWERS ARE SAYING ABOUT ZEPKE'S MOST HAUNTED SERIES...

"One of the things I really like about Terrance's book is that it is such an easy read. The tidbits of history keep you turning the pages, and you also learn about the paranormal investigators, who have used a variety of paranormal investigation tools...*A Ghost Hunter's Guide To The Most Haunted Places in America* is one of those books that keeps your imagination wondering what really happened."
    -Josh Schubert, **USA Travel Magazine**

"...*A Ghost Hunter's Guide To The Most Haunted Places in America*" explores the story behind these ghost story settings all throughout the country, from theatres, old factories, asylums, homes prisons, and much more. A Ghost Hunter's Guide To The Most Haunted Places in America is a must for lovers of the paranormal in America. Highly recommended.
    -James A. Cox, **Midwest Book Review**

"...while the words "adventure travel" may conjure up images of the remote or the foreign, a new book suggests that some wild rides are much closer to home. Zepke documents the supernatural in *A Ghost Hunter's Guide to the Most Haunted Houses in America*. As she points out, "Who else but an adventurous and brave soul would dare to spend time in a haunted dwelling—and pay good money to do so?"
    –Sarah Robbins, **Publishers Weekly**

"From a lunatic asylum to a brewery, ghostly presences inhabit all these places. Complete directions and site information is provided. Even if you don't get a chance to visit each of these locations, the stories and the black-and-white photos are fascinating.
    -Marcella Gauthier, **Escapees Magazine**

"You don't have to believe in ghosts to realize that certain places in our national history are haunted with legends and spirits of long ago. Terrance Zepke grew up in South Carolina knowing the tales of colonial pirates, Civil War legends, the impact of lowcountry voodoo, and the famous residents of weathered cemeteries...places you probably best not visit at night, She's written books such as *Coastal South Carolina: Welcome to the Lowcountry, Best Ghost Tales of South Carolina, Pirates of the Carolinas*, and her latest book, *A Ghost Hunter's Guide to the Most Haunted Places in America*, investigates saloons and cemeteries, former sanitariums, and penitentiaries across America where rumors of strange phenomenon seem to have some bearing...Terrance is one of the most schooled experts on paranormal in the United States."
　　–Rick Steves, ***Travel with Rick Steves***

"...From Georgia to California, Terrance writes about places that are home to a ghost or two -- and tells the horrible tales that led to these creatures remaining close to where they died. Her first chapter is about the Trans-Allegheny Lunatic Asylum in West Virginia, the place that creeped her out the most in her investigations into the paranormal -- and the one closest to where I live. It is told that many of the poor souls who died in the facility -- often from experimental treatments and procedures -- continue to roam the halls. Yawsa."
　　-Teresa Flatley, ***BoomThis! Magazine***

"...Zepke herself has always loved a good ghost story and heard many as she was growing up in the Carolinas. Now she has many books recording not only the stories she loves but also the history and photos of the places named. These places have all been investigated and proven haunted by the most sophisticated modern scientific equipment such as EMF detectors, which register electrical and magnetic fields, and EVP's (Electronic Voice Phenomenon), which digitally records sounds the human

ear cannot detect. Each place Zepke writes about has all the tour contact information also and many black and white photos. A fun way to plan a trip, if you aren't afraid!"
-Bonny Neely (**Top 1,000 Amazon Reviewer**)

"…a journalist by training, she [Zepke] takes you on a tour of the Trans-Allegheny Lunatic Asylum in West Virginia, the Birdcage Theatre in Arizona, and the Colonial Park Cemetery in Georgia, among a dozen other places…"
-Alan Caruba, **Bookviews.com** (National Book Critics Circle)

Featured on DadofDivas.com, Realtraveladventures.com, Charlotte Parent, LibraryThing.com, The TravelLady.com, Kayla's Reads & Reviews, Mature Life, Around the World, Goodreads, Carolina Parent, ConsumerTraveler.com, Prettyopinionated.com, 2BoomerBabes.com, Kidfriendly.com and National Public Radio.

Safari Publishing

All queries should be directed to: www.safaripublishing.net

Library of Congress Cataloging-in-Publication Data

Zepke, Terrance
A Ghost Hunter's Guide to The Most Haunted Houses in America/Terrance Zepke p. cm.

ISBN-10: 0985539832

ISBN-13: 978-0-9855398-3-2

1. Ghosts-America. 2. Haunted Houses-America. 3. Paranormal-America. I. Title.

First edition, April 2013

Cover Design by Michael Swing

A Ghost Hunter's Guide to The Most Haunted Houses in America

About the Author

Terrance Zepke loves ghost stories and travel. She has lived and traveled all over the world during her career as a freelance adventure travel writer. She has been to every continent and participated in all kinds of extraordinary adventures—from dog-sledding in the Arctic to spending the night in a haunted lunatic asylum (and many other creepy places). Even though she has lived in many great cities, such as Honolulu and London, she calls the Carolinas her "true home." She can't decide which state she likes best so she divides her time between North and South Carolina. She grew up in the South Carolina Lowcountry, which is what ignited her interest in ghosts. The Lowcountry is full of haunted places and tales of boo hags, hoodoo, and haints. She has written many books on the subject.

Introduction

I love a good ghost story, which explains why I have written so many books pertaining to the paranormal. This is the second book in my "most haunted" series. The first book focused on places, such as the Trans-Allegheny Lunatic Asylum and the St. Louis Cemetery.

This book addresses the most haunted houses in America. These houses were backdrops to all kinds of activity through the years, such as séances, slavery, suicide, murder, battle skirmishes, torture, voodoo, and more. No wonder they're full of lingering spirits!

Read on to discover why the Winchester House was built in such a bizarre manner—and why it is my favorite haunted house. Prepare to be horrified when you read the chapters on the Wolfe, LaLaurie, and Crenshaw houses. Judge for yourself if Amityville is indeed haunted or if it has been a huge hoax. See if you can figure out who brutally murdered the entire Moore family while reading about the Villisca House.

Learn who Yankee Jim was and why he won't leave Whaley House. Why did an exorcism have to be performed at the Hampton-Lillibridge House? Find out why demonologists believe there is something evil lurking in the barn at Prospect Place. Country music superstar Loretta Lynn shares her psychic gift, ghost stories, and even opens her haunted Hurricane Mills Plantation to the public.

I hope you enjoy reading *A Ghost Hunter's Guide to The Most Haunted Houses in America* as much as I enjoyed researching and writing it.

For more information on other books I've written and to check out my ghost gallery, visit www.terrancezepke.com. Also, be sure to take the fun quiz I've included at the end of the book to see if you're ready to chase these ghosts!

Winchester Mystery House

Winchester Mystery House

FUN FACTS:

*This four-story mansion started as a modest six-room house. It has six kitchens, 2,000 doors, and 10,000 windows. The house had seven stories before the Great Earthquake of 1906.

*No one knows for sure how many rooms are in it. Every count leads to a different total! It took the moving company six weeks to empty all the furniture out of the house after Sarah Winchester died because the men kept getting lost!

*There is one known "secret" passageway that is in the Séance Room. It is supposedly one of three exits from that room. It is believed that there are more secret passageways throughout the house that remain undiscovered after all these years. Also, Mrs. Winchester had spy panels installed throughout the house so that she could keep an eye on workmen and servants.

The History

Sarah Pardee was born in 1839 in New Haven, Connecticut. She grew up to be an attractive young woman, despite her tiny size. The 4'10" beauty was smart, fluent in several languages, possessed significant musical talents, and quite charming. She had many suitors, but finally settled on one when she was twenty-three years old. This may not seem old, but in the 1800s, it would have been unusual for a desirable woman not to have been married by that age.

Sarah Pardee married William Winchester on September 30, 1862. The Civil War had begun the previous year, so the whole country was in turmoil. But this didn't stop the couple from having a grand ceremony. Even though many were suffering terrible economic hardship due to the war, the Winchester family was not.

In fact, the affluent family became even more so during the war. That's because they owned an artillery company, which supplied soldiers with rifles. Most of the northern troops used their patented Henry rifle. The new state-of-the-art weapon could fire a shot every three seconds. It was the first repeating rifle and was the weapon of choice for Union soldiers. The Winchesters amassed a fortune from government contracts.

The year after the Civil War ended, Sarah gave birth to a baby girl. They named their daughter, Annie Pardee Winchester. Sarah and William were elated. They planned on having a large family. Little did they know at that time that she would be their only child.

Less than two weeks after she was born, the baby died from a rare, deadly disease known as "marasmus." The death of her newborn devastated Sarah. Her grief was so great that she suffered a mental breakdown, which went on for nearly ten years before she came to terms with her loss. Sadly, by the time that Sarah recovered, tragedy struck again.

Her beloved husband, William, died of tuberculosis. It was cold comfort that he had left her $20 million (Just imagine how much money that was back in 1881). Plus, Sarah inherited half of the highly profitable Winchester Repeating Arms Company.

But money can't buy happiness; at least it didn't for Sarah Winchester. She became so depressed that a concerned friend suggested she consult a medium. This led to another huge life change for Sarah. The medium told her that her dead husband, William, had communicated with her through this medium and that he had advised Sarah to leave New Haven forever. She needed a fresh start somewhere *far away*.

The medium added that her vision showed a curse had been placed on the Winchester family. "Many people have suffered and died because of your rifles. Their spirits are restless. You will never know peace," the woman predicted.

Believing every word of her prophecy, Sarah quickly packed and left Connecticut. She traveled across the country, not stopping until she reached California—as "far away" as she could get from Connecticut while remaining in the U.S. There she met a man who was building a modest six-room house. She convinced him to sell her the house and surrounding 160+ acres. She used the acreage to grow apricot and walnut trees. Revenue derived from the orchards added to her vast fortune. Wisely, Sarah also invested in other properties in Santa Clara Valley.

Sarah soon hired a large group of workmen to

work on the property. According to her whim on any given day, she ordered the men to build or demolish. This went on for thirty-eight years! That's because Sarah believed that if she ever stopped construction, she would die. On the other hand, if she kept building, she would have eternal life. It's unclear whether she was told this by a medium or came to this conclusion on her own.

Because of this firm belief, the woman kept men working on the house around the clock, 24/7—even on holidays. She had close to two dozen carpenters on payroll indefinitely. There was never a time that hammering, sawing, pounding, banging, and other common construction noises couldn't be heard. That alone would be enough to drive a person to insanity!

Sarah spent her days supervising the various crews and her nights sketching new building plans and communing with the spirit world. Because there were no formal building plans and Sarah had never studied architecture, the house ended up with a strange layout and many odd features.

There are hallways and stairs that lead nowhere. Some second-story doors open to the outside with nothing but a sharp drop to the ground below. There are three elevators and 47 fireplaces (some with incomplete chimneys). There is a 42-step staircase that only extends nine feet because the steps are only two inches high. There are doors joined to windows and closet doors that open to walls. Some bathrooms have glass instead of wood doors, while some stair posts were installed upside down. The number 13 is prevalent, from the number of panes in a window to the number of steps in most staircases.

But there may have been a method to her madness. Sarah may have believed that all these hallways and stairs leading nowhere would confuse the evil spirits.

(Stairs leading nowhere)

She may have thought that the number '13' was lucky, even though it is not normally considered to be a lucky

number. I believe that one of Sarah's spiritualists must have suggested that number. Why else would she use this number so often?

13 bathrooms

13 windows in the 13th bathroom

Most windows had 13 panes

13 hooks in the séance room (the hooks held different colored robes she wore during her regular séance sessions)

13 steps on most stairways

13 cupolas in the Greenhouse

13 ceiling panels in many rooms

*Sarah even had 13 sections in her will and signed the document 13 times!

Sarah filled her days working in the garden and overseeing contractors. She spent nights coming up with construction ideas, communing with spirits, and playing her baby grand piano. She was a talented musician, although few got to enjoy her performances since she kept to herself. Oddly, this lifestyle seemed to suit the widow.

In 1906, Sarah's world was again shattered. A great earthquake struck, all but destroying the mansion. The top three floors of the house collapsed. The fireplace collapsed in the room where she was sleeping; trapping her inside the room until workers could dig her out. (While Sarah had her own bedroom, she never slept in the same room more than one or two nights in a row. Supposedly, this was so that evil spirits could not find her during the night).

Reportedly, there were as many as 600 rooms before the quake. She took this destruction as a sign that the spirits were angry with her because construction was nearly done. She boarded up many of the rooms so that construction would never be complete.

Contractors got back to work after carrying off the debris. Almost hysterically, she ordered chimneys, bedrooms, and cupolas to be built. Visitors will see a little bit of everything throughout the home, except for mirrors. She did not permit mirrors in the house. There are only two mirrors in the mansion because she did not want to upset the ghosts she believed lived in the house. She set the table nightly to include place settings for her ghostly guests.

Sarah now held séances more frequently. On September 4, 1922 she went to bed after such an occasion and never woke up. The 83-year-old died in her sleep of heart failure. Her body was returned to New Haven, Connecticut for burial beside her husband, William Winchester. The estate had shrunk by the time she died because of the lengthy renovations and frequent consultations with mediums and spiritualists, but was still substantial. The furnishings were auctioned off and the house was sold to a group of investors. Today, it is a California Historical Landmark. Interestingly, the submission paperwork does not include an exact room count.

The Hauntings

It is widely believed to be haunted by many ghosts, including the ghost of Sarah Pardee Winchester. Some believe that it is haunted by the spirits of soldiers killed by Winchester rifles, who never gave Sarah a moment's peace. Numerous psychics and ghost hunting groups have investigated with mixed results. Some are convinced the dwelling is haunted while others are hesitant to officially declare it so. When Travel Channel's *Ghost Adventurers* conducted their investigation, Zak had to end it at 1 a.m. He got so freaked out that he called the property manager to come let them out immediately. This is the first and only time this has happened during their official investigations. Did the negative energy become too much for him or was there something else going on? We'll never know because he offered no explanation.

Whatever the cause, many visitors, workmen, and employees have heard footsteps and voices when no one is there; piano music is heard; chicken soup is sometimes smelled in the kitchen, which wasn't been operational in many years; strange balls of light are seen; cold spots have been experienced; windows bang for no reason; and firmly closed doors open seemingly on their own.

One of the bizarre events that has been reported many times is a huge ball of light that grows in size and moves around the room. It has been seen by ghost investigators and tour groups, but no one has captured it on film yet.

It is hard to say what the strangest part of this story is...Is it the design of the house or the hauntings or the enigma of Sarah herself? Perhaps it is the secrets the house still keeps, such as secret passageways and lingering spirits?

Any and all unusual incidents reported by visitors have been recorded on the Winchester House's official website. Most of the encounters occur in the Séance Room, basement, Sarah's bedroom, the gardens, the switchback staircase, and the Grand Ballroom.

Some believe that the switchback staircase is a portal or different portals to the other side. Many get claustrophobic, nauseas, and dizzy on it, but that may be due to its configuration rather than negative energy. The skinny staircase is comprised of five segments that twist and turn at odd angles and the ceiling is quite low above the stairwell.

Several years ago, an office manager reported seeing an old lady wearing Victorian-era clothes sitting in a chair in the dining room. She found the tour manager and told her that a new employee or volunteer was waiting for her in the dining room. The surprised woman went to the dining room to find out what was going on since she didn't have a clue what the other woman was talking about. The office manager followed her. When they got to the room where she had just left the woman waiting, there was no one there!

Visitor Information

525 S. Winchester Blvd.

San Jose, CA 95128

There are a variety of ways to explore this unique property. There are standard house tours, as well as flashlight tours, behind-the-scenes tours (includes the basement), garden tours, and fright nights.

San Jose is six hours from Los Angeles (351 miles); 8 hours from Las Vegas, Nevada (533 miles); and 27 hours from Houston, TX (1,887 miles).

www.winchestermyseryhouse.com

(A visitor took this picture in 2005. This was Sarah's favorite area in her gardens. Is this a photo anomaly or is this the spirit of Sarah still enjoying her gardens?)

In its heyday, the gardens were spectacular. Sarah employed a minimum of eight gardeners. She imported all kinds of exotic plants, shrubs, trees, flowers, and herbs from around the world. Visitors will appreciate 100-year-old rose bushes, enormous ferns, and spectacular fan date palms. In keeping with all of the owner's eccentricities, the gardeners were instructed to maintain a hedge around the entire house. This hedge was so tall that only the top part of the house was visible from the road. Mrs. Winchester valued her privacy. Reportedly, she fired a servant who saw her without her veil. (Reportedly, she only appeared in public in later years wearing a veil). She rarely left the house, except to enjoy her gardens from the vantage point of her lovely gazebos. Upon her death in 1922, the grounds were opened to the public as Winchester Park. The entire estate underwent extensive renovations beginning in 1973. Part of the renovations included major plantings. Roughly 1,500 shrubs, trees, and plants were added. Also, 12,000 hedges were planted along the pathways throughout the garden.

Crenshaw "Old Slave" House

Crenshaw "Old Slave" House

FUN FACTS:

The structure was a station on the Reverse Underground Railroad.

The attic runs the length of the house and contains a dozen rooms that are believed to have been constructed for or converted into secret slave cells.

There was a tunnel that ran from the basement to the Saline River so that Crenshaw could transport slaves during the night to reduce the risk of getting caught participating in this illegal activity.

The History

John Hart Crenshaw was born in 1797 near Wilmington, North Carolina. When he was a boy, his father, William Crenshaw, moved the family out West to seek his fortune. Instead of fortune, they found

hardship. The Crenshaw home was annihilated by an earthquake in 1811. The family moved again, this time to southern Illinois because William Crenshaw had heard that a large salt deposit had been discovered. Excitedly, he leased land from the government and started a salt refinery. He called his new venture,

Half Moon Lick. William Crenshaw died soon after he got the business up and running. This left his oldest son, John, in charge of everything. In addition to the growing business, John was responsible for his mother and six siblings. Salt production was hard work and so was the custodianship of his entire family, but John handled the challenges well.

By 1830 the government decided to sell all the land they had leased for salt mining in order to raise funds for a much needed prison. Lease holders were given first chance to buy their land. John Hart Crenshaw bought his land, as well as thousands of additional acres over the next several years. Although John Crenshaw was a despicable person, he was a hard worker and savvy businessman. In addition to his farm, he owned a saw mill and several salt mines.

It is important to note how valuable salt was in those days. It was considered more important than gold or silver. Salt was necessary both to keep food from spoiling and as a vital nutrient. Salt was so vital that certain laws were overlooked in order to aid production. Slavery was illegal in Illinois. However, it was nearly impossible to find free men willing to tackle such back-breaking work. So the state made Crenshaw exempt from the anti-slavery law. He was allowed to have as many slaves as he needed to work the salt mines. Records indicate he had as many as 750 slaves in 1830. Crenshaw engaged in other illegal activities, such as using night riders and leasing slaves (see below for more information).

Why would the government ever allow such a

thing? *Taxes.* Almost ten percent of Illinois revenue was derived from the tax money that Crenshaw paid on his business enterprises and land.

John Crenshaw decided to build a home that was on par with his affluence. In 1833, he hired an architect and began work on his dream house, Hickory Hill. It took several years for the large, three-story pseudo-Greek Revival style house to be completed. But it was worth the wait. The two-story edifice was exactly what John Crenshaw had wanted. There was a fireplace in most rooms and the outside of the house featured large columns, wide verandahs, and sweeping balconies. John and his wife collected antiques and artwork from all over Europe to fill his large home.

The attic ran the length of the house and contained a dozen rooms that are believed to have been constructed for or converted into secret slave cells. He had two whipping posts in the attic. Slaves were held here until buyers were found and arrangements made. Then they were taken to the basement. Allegedly, there was a tunnel that ran from the basement to the Saline River so that he could transport slaves during the night. This is how Hickory Hill came to be known as the "Old Slave House."

Crenshaw also conducted a practice known as "night riding." He hired men to go riding at night to find escaped slaves. The runaway slaves were captured by Crenshaw's men and taken to his attic. They were subsequently ransomed back to their owners or returned for a reward. But the most unspeakable thing he did was to kidnap free men, women, and children and sell them into slavery. The Underground Railroad had "stations" to help escaped slaves find freedom. Crenshaw and many others who engaged in night riding created a Reverse Underground Railroad whereby they captured freed slaves and sold them into slavery.

Ironically, one of the biggest opponents of slavery slept on the floor below the slave holding cells. When Abraham Lincoln was a state representative, he attended a debate and ball held in the Crenshaw House. It was late when the fete ended and many guests, including Lincoln, spent the night. Assuredly, no slaves were transported that night!

As they say, what goes around comes around. Word got around about his shady business activities. He was in and out of court for several years. He lost his standing as a "pillar of the community."

Crenshaw was arrested and indicted in the 1820s for kidnapping a (free) black woman and her children. Maria Adams and her eight children ended up in Texas as slaves. He was arrested another time for the same crime but the outcome is not documented. He was arrested again in 1828 when he sold sixteen men into slavery in Tennessee. That same year, he kidnapped a woman and her children and sold them into slavery in Kentucky. He kidnapped four men in the 1840s and sold them into slavery in Arkansas, but they were set free after the discovery. It is unknown how many other men, women, and children he kidnapped and sold into slavery but was never caught or convicted of those crimes.

In addition to his legal woes, his financial empire

began to crumble. His sawmill was destroyed by fire, but it was never revealed whether the fire was accidental or arson. His final demise came when substantial salt deposits were found in Ohio and Virginia. Demand for salt mining in Illinois plummeted.

Crenshaw's behavior finally caught up to him. He got a dose of what he had been dispensing for years. According to legend, a slave witnessed him beating a woman in the fields one afternoon. The irate man picked up a nearby ax and charged at Crenshaw. The sharp tool severed Crenshaw's leg when it struck him, causing him to lose most of the leg.

Crenshaw was barely holding on financially when the Civil War broke out. During the war, he sold Hickory Hill and moved to a little farmhouse in another town. He lived there quietly until his death on December 4, 1871. He was buried at Hickory Hill Cemetery, near his old homestead.

Hickory Hill became famous in the early 1900s when it was bought by the Sisk family and opened to the public. As stories spread about paranormal activity occurring in the old house, people began knocking on the door asking if they could have a tour. This is how the Sisk family came to begin charging admission and giving tours of their home.

(The house as it appears today).

The Hauntings

How did it come to gain its reputation as a haunted house? The Sisk family claimed to hear strange noises in the attic, ranging from chains rattling to cries and moans.

Ghost hunters wanted more than a tour. They wanted to stay in the haunted house. So, the Sisk family let adventurous souls stay in the attic overnight for a fee. No one ever made it through the night, so the legend of the Old Slave House grew. Lots of overnight visitations were now taking place. The overnight stays ended when some people got so scared that they knocked over a lantern and started a fire while fleeing the attic in the middle of the night.

The tourist attraction was shut down by the Sisk family in 1996 due to old age and bad health. The state bought the property in 2000. In 2004, the National Park Service included the property as a "station" on the Reverse Underground Railroad.

During tours, some visitors have suddenly felt very cold or nauseas or melancholy for no good reason. Some have been touched by an unseen presence.

Visitor Information

The Crenshaw House is fourteen miles east of Harrisburg, Illinois at the junctions of Highway 45 and 13. The closest town is Equality. The place is closed to the public and it remains uncertain what will become of the historic property. There are no plans to re-open the property due to a lack of funding. Signs are posted warning trespassers that they will be prosecuted if caught.

Harrisburg is ten miles from Equality, IL; 4.5 hours from Cincinnati, OH (275 miles); and 5.5 hours from Chicago, IL (340 miles).

Hampton-Lillibridge House

Hampton-Lillibridge House

FUN FACTS:

The owner had an exorcism performed on this house on December 6, 1963. It did not help and he ultimately had to move out of the haunted dwelling.

The lead character in the bestselling book that was later made into a movie, *Midnight in the Garden of Good and Evil*, is based on the owner of this house, Jim Williams.

This house has an unusual history. It was moved from its original location. A workman was killed in the process. It was built on top of a crypt. It became many things over the years, including a tenement where a man killed himself.

The History

This house, built in 1796, looks a tad out of place among all the Revival and Colonial architectural-style homes that are typical for this area. Since it was built for Rhode Island native, Hampton Lillibridge, the Cape Cod design makes perfect sense. The New Englander insisted on a widow's walk at the top of the house, which is a classic Cape Cod feature.

During the Great Fire of 1820, many buildings throughout Savannah were destroyed. This house remains one of a handful of structures that survived, making it all the more significant. It has been bought and sold many times throughout the years, the first time being right after Hampton Lillibridge's death. For many years, it served as a boarding house and later a tenement. Legend has it that a young sailor hanged himself in his room.

The property became run down due to neglect. No telling what would have happened to it if not for Jim Williams. His primary occupation was an antiques dealer, but he was also a restoration enthusiast. He bought and renovated several properties in historic Savannah, including this three-story house he bought in 1963.

He also bought the house next door. At that time, these two residences were located on East Bryan Street.

Once Jim assumed ownership, he had them moved to East Julian Street. Sadly, the second property did not survive the move. It fell apart during transit, killing one of the workmen involved in the project.

More bad news came when the contractor discovered a crypt as the crew was securing the house onto the foundation. They stopped work and reported it to Jim Williams. They revealed their findings and asked what he wanted to do. He quizzed them for a few minutes, specifically about what was in the crypt. The men told their employer that it was full of water so they didn't know for sure. However, they assumed it was empty. Williams chose not to investigate any further. He told the construction workers to leave the crypt alone and get back to work.

As soon as the work was completed on the house, Jim Williams moved in. He was so excited about his new home that he could barely sleep the week he moved in. He had no idea how his life was about to change—for the worse.

 The Hauntings

Throughout the project, the contractors witnessed weird events. They heard footsteps on the second floor but never found anyone when they ran up to investigate. There was no other exit, so they were baffled as to what was going on. They also heard soft, but distinct, voices. Again, when they went upstairs or into the next room to check it out, they never found anything.

But those things were nothing compared to the sightings. Even the biggest naysayer was forced to admit something supernatural was going on when they began seeing apparitions in the window. Two different ghosts were reported. One was a gray-haired man sporting a gray suit or robe. The other appeared as a tall, dark figure in black or dark-colored coloring. Whenever a brave soul darted inside to catch the intruder, there was no one there.

There were other witnesses to paranormal activity besides the workmen. Several of Jim's neighbors reported seeing shadowy figures in the windows. They saw lights and activity that mimicked a party—figures dancing and singing in the downstairs living room. This really spooked the neighbors since it always happened when Jim was out of town on a buying trip. If there was nobody home, who turned on the lights and what was the deal with the music, singing, and figures dancing?

The neighbors reported these unexplainable events to Jim Williams time and time again. He thanked them for letting him know, but ignored what he was told. Presumably, he did so because he didn't know what to do about it and hoped it might work itself out.

But it didn't. In fact, things got worse. Williams couldn't keep a maid. They seldom lasted more than a few weeks or months before quitting. They always said the same thing. They were sorry, but they couldn't work in this kind of environment. They were frightened by the things they were seeing and hearing in the house. Jim still didn't know how to handle the situation, so he continued to ignore it. Finally, one autumn afternoon Jim Williams was forced to address what was happening in his beloved home.

Jim had a few friends over. Everyone was on the first floor socializing, when a loud noise was heard overhead. One of the guests bolted up the stairs to catch the prankster. Jim called after the man to stop him. His guest ignored his request and continued his sprint up the stairs. He soon disappeared from view and there was no noise of any kind coming from the second floor. The group stood at the bottom of the stairs and yelled to the missing man. They pleaded with him to answer them, to let them know he was all right. After calling out several times, they group collectively ventured upstairs. They were shocked at what they found.

The man was lying in a crumpled heap on the floor. He was face down and not moving. They turned him over and helped him sit up. He was unable to speak for several minutes. Finally, he explained what had happened. The man said that as soon as he started down the hallway, it suddenly got very cold. He felt as if he was in a cold body of water. As he was pondering this sensation, he was dragged by an unseen presence down the hall towards one of the bedrooms. He struggled with all his might. His efforts were rewarded when he was abruptly discarded by his invisible assailant. He was literally too frightened to move. This had all transpired just before they found him.

After this encounter, friends stopped coming around. They were afraid of being attacked or just felt too spooked to relax here. Jim knew he had to do something. While he was still deciding how to proceed, he saw a ghostly figure in the doorway of his bedroom one evening. The apparition entered the room and approached the bed. It disappeared less than three or four feet away from the bed.

This happened on another occasion, but Williams took action this time. He jumped out of bed and headed towards the spirit. The figure quickly exited the room and disappeared down the hall. Jim bolted after it, determined to get answers. The figure disappeared into one of the other bedrooms. Williams followed, but found the door was locked! This got to Jim more than anything that had happened so far. From then on, he kept a gun in his bedside table. Wonder how Jim thought a bullet was going to stop a ghost?

The harassed homeowner turned to the church for help. He set an appointment for December 7, 1963. Bishop Albert Rhett Stewart of the Episcopal Diocese performed both an exorcism and a traditional blessing upon the home. An exorcism is the "religious practice of evicting demons or other spiritual entities from a person or place. Exorcisms were rare until the 1900s. After that, they became an acceptable practice, especially during the early 1960s through the mid-1970s.

For several days following the exorcism, there was no activity. Jim Williams was convinced that his home was once again a safe and happy environment. But then a maid complained of an unexplainable rattling noise, like a chain. She also claimed to sense a supernatural presence in the house. Neighbors saw and heard party activity at the house when no one was home.

The Rhine Research Center (formerly known as the Paranormal Center at Duke University) conducted an official investigation. They found the dwelling to be haunted. Legendary ghost hunter, Hans Holzer, also decreed the place as haunted. Many psychics, including Dr. William Roll of the American Psychical Research Foundation, also weighed in. After spending a few nights there, he declared the house to be "the most psychically possessed property in the nation."

Jim threw in the towel. There was nothing else he could do. He moved out in late spring 1964. The house has changed ownership many times since then. All the owners have reported strange activity, but none have been harmed or unduly harassed. The most common complaints are the footsteps overheard, the sounds of objects (furniture) being moved, and the feeling that they are sharing their residence with one or more ghosts.

Lowcountry legend has it that if you paint porches, steps, window frames, and/or doors on your home 'Indigo Blue,' it will prevent evil spirits from entering. If you get a chance to visit Savannah and see this property, you'll notice that one of the owners has painted the underside of the porch 'Indigo Blue.'

Visitor Information

The house is located at 507 E. Julian Street. It is a private residence and not open to the public. However, it can clearly be seen from the street and sidewalk that extends alongside the property.

Midnight in the Garden of Good and Evil was written

by John Berendt. The book put Savannah on the map and still plays an important role today. It was published in 1994 and remained on the bestseller list for 216 weeks. The novel was made into a popular movie. The success is due partly to the eclectic characters, such as Lady Chablis and Hoodoo priestess, Miranda. The story is loosely based on incredible real life events that happened in the 1980s that involved Jim Williams. The garden of good and evil refers to Bonaventure Cemetery. The famous Bird Girl statue from the book jacket was relocated from the cemetery to the Telfair Museum in 1997.

Savannah is four hours from Charlotte, NC and Atlanta, GA (250 miles); and 6 hours from Chattanooga, TN (366 miles).

Whaley House

Whaley House

FUN FACTS:

The structure has served as a theater, reception hall, courtroom, recital hall, and private residence.

It cost $10,000 to build in the mid-1800s.

It took Thomas Whaley 204 days to travel from New York to California. He came by boat and there were a lot of problems en route, including storms, rough seas, and a leaky vessel. When he arrived in San Francisco, there were already 150 vessels in port. They were full of men who had come West to seek their fortune.

The History

The house was built by Thomas Whaley Jr. The project took more than two years to complete. Whaley was a native New Yorker who had been lured to California by the Gold Rush, like many other men across America.

San Francisco was reacting quickly to the needs of its new residents. Tents were thrown up as "stores" and flimsy buildings served as saloons. Tom Whaley soon set up a store on Montgomery Street. Hoping to make his fortune, he sold hardware supplies and miner's equipment on consignment.

His business was such a success that he soon moved to a nicer building and eventually bought his own building that included office space and a living area above the store. He made enough money to buy land and build a nice two-story house overlooking the bay. And then tragedy struck.

A fire blazed through the city the first week of May 1851. Many structures, including Whaley's store, were destroyed. He made the decision not to rebuild. Instead, he left San Francisco and headed for San Diego. Four months later he was settled in his new hometown. The small Spanish town was nothing like San Francisco. For one thing, the population of San Diego was only 250 or so. For another, there wasn't much commerce. There was one apothecary shop, two hotels, and six stores.

Once again, Whaley had good luck with his business. It did so well that he went back East and married Anna De Launay, who had been waiting for him to claim his fortune and come back for her.

Whaley spent two years building his dream house. He boasted that it was the best house in San Diego. Indeed, the two-story edifice on San Diego Avenue was impressive. One of the nicest features was the five doors across the front of the house. The lower part was wood and the upper consisted of large window panes.

By this time, Thomas and Anna had two children. Frank was born in 1854 and Anna Amelia in 1858. Sadly, Frank died approximately five months after Anna Amelia was born.

A fire broke out two months later, which burned down Thomas's store. The final straw came when an earthquake of great magnitude struck San Diego on May 27, 1862. Many buildings were damaged and destroyed. The Whaley family was visiting friends in San Francisco when they got the news that their home had been badly damaged.

Thomas and Anna had three more children: George, Violet, and Corinne. They eventually returned to San Diego and made the necessary repairs to their home, which included expansions to comfortably accommodate all the children.

Thomas died on December 14, 1890. His youngest daughter, Corinne, lived in the house until her death in 1953. She lived to a ripe old age of eighty-nine years old. Her journal reveals that she was frightened by a sinister presence in the upstairs bedrooms. She may have lived here until her death, but she never felt "secure" in the house.

The Whaley House deteriorated over the years to a sad state of disrepair. The house was bought by the Board of Supervisors of San Diego in 1956 and restorations began.

 The Hauntings

Whaley House has been declared officially haunted by the U.S. Commerce Department, an honor shared with only one other house in America—Winchester House (which is also discussed in this book).

EVPs often pick up the sound of a gavel being banged, as in a judge calling a court to order or rendering a verdict.

Cigar smoke is often smelled but smoking is not permitted. The smell of lingering perfume is sometimes detected. The sounds of a piano being played are heard on occasion and objects are often found out of place.

There are lots of popular theories as to who

haunts this dwelling. Some believe it is haunted by two of the children. Thomas and Anna had six children, but two died of childhood illness and suicide. Some speculate it's haunted by those who were killed here. The house was built on the site of execution gallows. Some of those who had been executed were mostly likely buried here in unmarked graves.

Sightings of Anna, while uncommon, have occurred over the years. Famous TV personality and entertainer, Regis Philbin, swore he saw her. He and his wife and several other credible witnesses visited the house in November 1964. The plan had been to spend the night but everyone left after seeing the apparition.

The second floor is the most active. Visitors and investigators have reported seeing silhouettes, shadows, and people. Thousands of photos taken over the years show a shape in the courtroom believed to be Yankee Jim looking out the kitchen window. Yankee Jim was one of many who was tried and convicted and executed here.

Yankee Jim Robinson was tried in the courtroom at Whaley House. He was badly injured and had no counsel, yet he was found guilty and sentenced to death. He was hanged in the yard behind the house. Many have seen his spirit roaming the halls of Whaley House.

Famed ghost hunter, Hans Holzer, investigated Whaley House and declared that it was haunted by Thomas Whaley. Holzer saw a figure at the top of the stairs that he said resembled the patriarch. Authors, psychics, reporters, researchers, and ghost hunters have all investigated the property over the years. Most agree that it is definitely haunted.

Perhaps it is best summed up by Susan Michaels, Author of *Sightings: Beyond Imagination Lies the Truth.* In this publication she states "There's an invisible energy that exists between magnet and metal. You can't see it or touch it, but you know it's there. There is growing evidence that people generate the same kind of magnetic energy and that this energy remains in the environment even after death. You can't see it or touch it, but you know it's there. The term is used to describe haunting in which energy from the past is seen in the form of apparitions or heard as ghostly sounds. In a residue [residual] haunting, these spiritual energies do not interact with the living; instead, they are echoes in time replaying over and over like an old movie."

Visitor Information

2482 San Diego Avenue

San Diego, CA 92110

It was converted into a museum in 1960. It is open to the public. Daytime and evening tours are offered.

San Diego is two hours from Long Beach, CA (111 miles); 6 hours from Phoenix, AZ (400 miles); and 8 hours from San Francisco, CA (500 miles).

www.whaleyhouse.org

Villisca Axe Murder House

Villisca Axe Murder House

FUN FACTS:

The eight murders that took place here occurred a few days after the sinking of the *Titanic*. It was such big news that it knocked the shipwreck off the front page of most newspapers.

This is a small, sleepy town these days, but back in the early 1900s, it was a thriving place. The population was more than 2,500 and dozens of trains stopped in Villisca, which resulted in a lot of business development.

The Moores were respected and liked by the whole community. Even today, many townspeople feel it is disrespectful to their memory to allow tourists and ghost investigators into their former home.

The History

June 10, 1912. For most of us, this date holds no significance. But for one community, it remains the most memorable date in the town's history—even more than 100 years later.

Here are the names and ages of the family members involved in this story:

Josiah "J.B." Moore (father, Age 43)

Sarah Moore (mother, Age 39)

Herman Moore (son, Age 11)

Katherine Moore (daughter, Age 10)

Boyd Moore (son, Age 7)

Paul Moore (son, Age 5)

Lena Stillinger (friend, Age 12), came home from church with family and spent the night

Ina Stillinger (friend, Age 8), came home from church with family and spent the night

The story begins in Villisca, Iowa on June 9, 1912. The Moore family attended a special church service, which ended about 9:30 p.m. They invited the Stillinger sisters to spend the night. They returned to the Moore house and enjoyed milk and cookies before going to bed. The Stillinger girls slept downstairs while the rest of the family went upstairs to their bedrooms. What happened next remains the biggest unsolved murder mystery in Iowa.

The next morning a neighbor, Mary Peckham, noticed that there was no activity at the Moore house. This was unusual because the family normally awoke very early to begin their chores. By mid-morning, the neighbor was very concerned because the chickens hadn't even been let out of their coop and there was no sign of anyone. No one answered the door when she knocked. She tried to open the door but it was locked.

Mary Peckham contacted Josiah Moore's brother, Ross Moore, who came to the house. He banged on the door with his fist repeatedly and shouted their names. When there was no answer at the front or back doors, he used his spare key to enter the house.

Immediately, he realized that the house was too quiet. He did not hear or see any activity. This was remarkable given that there should be two adults and six children on the premises. He soon discovered the reason why. He found the bodies of two little girls. He recognized them as being Lena and Ina Stillinger. They had been bludgeoned to death. Horrified, Ross Moore hurried through the house where he found the entire Moore family had also been bludgeoned to death in their sleep. They had been savagely attacked with an axe.

Ross Moore immediately called for Sheriff Hank Horton to come to the scene of the crime. A physician was summoned too. So what happened between 10 p.m. when the family went to sleep and the next morning? It was determined that the murders most likely occurred between midnight and 2 a.m. on June 10. The sheriff believes that the first to be murdered were the parents. Josiah Moore suffered a particularly brutal murder. Then the Moore children were killed. Lastly, the killer made his way downstairs and murdered the two Stillinger sisters.

The authorities determined that Lena Stillinger was probably awake during her attack as they found defensive wounds on her arm. Also, it was discovered that the door was locked from the inside, so how did the killer enter and exit the property? And why did he start his killing spree on the second floor rather than the first floor? How is it that no screams or cries were heard? One theory is that there was a train that comes through town nightly at 2 a.m. and the killer timed the crime to coincide with the noisy train.

There will never be answers to these questions because the evidence was contaminated, to say the least. Many believe that it remains an unsolved crime because the local authorities botched the investigation. Reportedly, hundreds of people walked through the house, touching things and even removing items as souvenirs. Supposedly, one man walked off with part of Josiah's skull! The National Guard arrived that afternoon and secured the property, but so much damage had been done by then that it was too late.

What emerged during the course of the investigation is incredible. Several suspects came to light:

William Mansfield. He was believed to be the hit man hired by Frank F. Jones (see below). Mansfield was unstable. He used drugs and was a known killer for hire.

Reverend George Kelly was a traveling preacher. He was a creepy-looking man who was prone to wild rants. Also, he was believed to be a "Peeping Tom" and was at the church the night of the June 9. Furthermore, he suddenly left town the morning of June 10. He confessed to the crimes saying that he had a vision to do it. But there was not enough proof to arrest him. However, he was arrested two years later for sending pornography through the mail. He was sent to a mental hospital. Oddly, he was arrested five years after the murders for committing the murders. He made no sense when put on the stand during the trial and he had recanted his confession prior to the trial. This resulted in a hung jury. He was retried and acquitted in a second trial.

Andy Sawyer was believed to a serial killer responsible for the Moore murders, as well as several other murders that occurred in the Midwest within months of Villisca House murders. He was often seen toting an ax and acting strangely. He seemed to know a lot about the crimes and was a transient, so he made a good suspect. He was arrested but there was not enough proof so he was released. He disappeared shortly thereafter.

Henry Moore had the same last name but was not related to the family. He was also a transient. Six months after the Villisca killings, Moore was convicted of murdering his mother and grandmother in Missouri. He bludgeoned them with an ax. It is believed that he committed more than twenty murders in five states over the course of eighteen months. Two of those murders were Rollin Hudson and his wife. They were brutally murdered just four days before the Villisca killings. A federal investigator who was assigned to the case, James McClaughry, believed that this mentally-impaired transient was responsible. The Fed was convinced that the Hudson family, Moore family, Wayne family, and Burnham family were all done by Henry Moore—a total of 23 murders.

More than a year later, the police hired a private detective to investigate. The detective, James Wilkerson with the Burns Detective Agency (Kansas City), came up with a new theory. He accused a local businessman who was also a state senator, **Frank F. Jones**, of hiring a hit man, **William Mansfield**, to kill Josiah Moore. Wilkerson believes Mansfield decided to kill the rest of the family even though he was only hired to get rid of Josiah Moore. Moore worked for Jones before starting his own business, which was a John Deere franchise. This hurt Jones financially, but was it worth murdering his family over? The rumors that Moore was having an affair with Jones' daughter-in-law, Dona, may have been enough to push him and his son, **Albert Jones**, to punish Moore for his alleged affair with Albert's wife. But there was no proof of any wrongdoing. The detective's theories were discredited and the case was dismissed.

So what was the outcome? A $3,500 reward was offered "for the arrest and conviction of the murderer or murderers of J.B. Moore and family and Lena and Ina Stillinger at Villisca on the night of Sunday, June 9, 1912, the state of Iowa, Montgomery county, citizens of the city of Villisca, and the adjoining community offer a reward approximating $3,500." No one was ever convicted of these crimes. Since the person was never caught, the reward money was used instead to purchase gravestones for the Moore family. Officially, the case remains open and unsolved more than 100 years later.

The Hauntings

There have been many occupants of the house since 1910. In 1930, Homer and Bonnie Ritter rented the house. Every night, Bonnie awoke to find a man standing at the foot of the bed holding an ax. Homer never saw the man but heard someone walking around downstairs and climbing the stairs. He never found anyone when he went to investigate. The Ritters soon moved out of the house.

Linda Cloud and her sister, Patti, lived there with their parents and siblings when they were growing up. At that time, they did not know the history of the property. They both heard voices and heard a girl crying. They both returned to their former home a couple of years ago. Patti got so upset during the visit to the house that she had to leave. Both women said that an unbearable feeling of sadness overcame them when they were inside the house.

Darwin and Martha Linn bought the property in the 1990s. They are residents of Villisca and already own a museum in town. They made extensive renovations both because of the condition of the old house and also to restore it to its original appearance (as much as possible). This made it suitable to be on the National Register of Historic Places. The house has been made to look like it did when the Moore family lived there, including period antiques and furnishings.

Sadly, the original artifacts are long done, but the Linns did a good job of recreating the setting. It became a museum house and is open to daylight tours. It is also available overnight for paranormal investigators. Over the years, many weird things have been reported. These include the sounds of children's voices and laughter when no children are on site. Tour groups have witnessed moving objects and banging noises. Some overnight guests have reported a "ghostly fog." It is a creepy fog that suddenly appears and moves from room to room and eventually disappears.

The next door neighbor feels that a demonic presence is inside the house. Many feel a dark energy or evil presence in the house. Ghost hunters have been attacked by an unseen force. Most feel that the spirit of the murderer remains in the house. Many believe that residual and intelligent hauntings are occurring here.

Visitor Information

The house is open year round for tours during the days. Individuals and groups may rent the house overnight. It stays booked up almost every night during the summer months. Most ghost groups do leave with mysterious EVPs and abnormal EMF detector readings.

508 2nd Street

Villisca, Iowa 50864

Villisca is two hours from Lincoln, NE (111 miles); 2.5 hours from Kansas City, KS (148 miles); and 11 hours from Nashville, TN (705 miles).

www.villiscaiowa.com

Loretta Lynn Plantation House

Loretta Lynn Plantation House

FUN FACTS:

A Civil War battle took place on the grounds of this former plantation.

Loretta Lynn possesses psychic abilities, which she believes she inherited from her mother.

Loretta Lynn has owned the property since 1967. Nearly every member of her family has reported paranormal experiences.

Loretta Lynn, 2005 Concert

The History

Loretta Lynn is known as the "Queen of Country." She has produced 54 studio records, 15 compilation albums, one tribute album for her idol Patsy Cline, and 88 singles during her music career. Her first hit was "Honky Tonk Girl." Since then, more than five million of her records have sold. A blockbuster movie was made about her life, Coal Miner's Daughter.

In addition to her impressive resume, she's also a psychic and owns a haunted house. She is the owner of a former plantation located in Hurricane Mills, Tennessee. The town, dating back to 1810, was built around an iron furnace. In the early 1800s, a Masonic Temple and a church with a cemetery were built here. These buildings were used as a hospital during the Civil War. A skirmish occurred here on July 22, 1863. Nineteen soldiers died that day. They were buried on the grounds in the church cemetery.

When the iron ran out in the 1850s, a flour mill was built in 1876 by James Anderson, although some sources report Mills Plantation wasn't built until the 1890s. Loretta Lynn bought the house in 1966 and lived there until 1984. At that time, the house was converted into a museum. The former flour mill is now a peanut farm. Some of the land is leased to farmers who grow corn and have cows. The Masonic Temple and cemetery still exist.

When she bought the place, Loretta Lynn was at the peak of her career. So, she was on tour most of the time. But with the help of her husband, "Doo," Loretta raised six children in this house.

When her mother came to visit for the first time, Loretta took her mother on a tour of the property. When they got to the river, Loretta's mother gasped. Alarmed at a vision that had suddenly popped into her head, she told Loretta that a family tragedy was going to happen here. And it did. Several years later, Loretta's oldest son, Jack Benny, mysteriously drowned in the Duck River. When her husband tried to break the news to her, she said, "It's Jack Benny, isn't it?" before he could get the words out. She did not recover fully from the terrible seizure she suffered at the exact moment of his death until his body was found a few days later. That was in 1984.

After Jack Benny's death, she converted the house into a museum. Loretta added a replica of her childhood home in Kentucky, which was made famous in the movie, Coal Miner's Daughter. "Doo" died in 1996. Although Loretta no longer resides in Mills Plantation, she does live in another house located on the same property.

The Hauntings

Loretta Lynn may be the perfect channel for the spirits that linger at Hurricane Mills Plantation. She is a psychic, a gift she believes she inherited from her mother. Loretta says that she saw her father in a coffin in a vision. The next day she learned he died of a massive stroke at the same moment she had the vision. She saw the ghost of her father when she returned to her childhood home shortly thereafter.

She believes that one of the spirits that haunt the house is former owner, James Anderson. Another spirit that has been seen by many over the years is the "Woman in White." She usually appears in a doorway. Her twins, Peggy and Patsy, saw the "Woman in White" many times when they were children. They saw her at the foot of their beds and in the doorway of the bathroom. She has shown herself to Loretta too. One day when Loretta returned home from a concert tour, she saw a woman wearing a white dress standing on the second floor balcony. She appeared to be crying. Loretta hurried upstairs to find out who this woman was and what was wrong. There was no one there when she got to the balcony. The woman had simply vanished! Later, she discovered a grave marker for Beaulah Anderson and one for her child. According to the headstones, Beaulah died twelve days after giving birth to a stillborn baby. Legend has it she died of a broken heart. Loretta is convinced that the woman she saw on the balcony is Beaulah Anderson, still mourning the loss of her baby.

There may be slave spirits too. A pit has been discovered underneath the porch. There are hooks and chains still in it. It appears that slaves were punished in this pit. Family members and visitors have heard the sounds of chains rattling, dragging sounds across the porch, and unexplained footsteps.

But there's another possibility. There is an old iron bridge on the grounds and what appears to be a small group of Confederate soldiers has been seen standing on this bridge, as well as elsewhere on the grounds. These may be the restless spirits of the nineteen soldiers who were killed during battle on July 22, 1863.

The most haunted room in the entire house is the Brown Room. This is one of the upstairs bedrooms. The first thing visitors notice is how much colder this room is than the rest of the house. Loretta's personal assistant, Tim Cobb, claims to have seen a shadowy figure in the room late one afternoon as he passed by it.

When he stopped and went inside to investigate, he found no one. Loretta's oldest son, Jack Benny, had a creepy encounter in the Brown Room in 1968. He laid down late one afternoon to rest. He was stretched out on top of the bed cover fully dressed. He awoke when he felt a tugging. When he looked in the direction it was coming from, he saw a Confederate soldier removing his boots. His brother, Ernest, also had a Brown Room experience. He awoke to find two Confederate soldiers at the foot of the bed. That was the last time anyone slept in the Brown Room.

Another "hot spot" seems to be the staircase. Loretta's albums have been framed and hang on the wall at the stairwell. None of the employees or visitors is allowed to touch them. Instructions are given about this at the start of any tour. One time a tour guide touched an album as she explained this policy. She was pushed down the stairs by an unseen force. One of the tour participants claimed to have seen a male figure behind her on the staircase just before he fell down several steps. The morning after this happened, a manager found all the albums turned to the wall.

Three employees were locked on the balcony one day. They were on the balcony hanging banners promoting a special event. Suddenly, the doors closed and locked on their own. The women were stuck on the balcony until someone finally rescued them.

Visitor Information

The 3,500-acre Hurricane Mills is one of the leading tourist attractions in Tennessee. It is the 12th most visited place, ranking above Ruby Falls and the Jack Daniels Distillery. More than a half million visitors come to see the village, which is considered "heritage tourism." The self-guided tour includes the 18,000-square foot museum. In addition to touring the house and ground, there are campgrounds, a pool, paddle boats, canoeing, fishing, an RV park, horseback riding, concerts, and other special events.

8000 Hwy. 13 South

Hurricane Mills, TN 37078

Hurricane Mills is 4 hours from Knoxville, TN (255 miles); 8 hours from Columbia, SC (530 miles; and 10 hours from Raleigh, NC (600 miles).

www.lorettalynnranch.net

(This is Loretta Lynn's former home in Butcher Hollow, Kentucky).

Amityville House

Amityville House

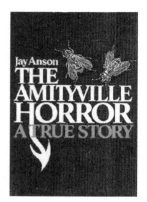

FUN FACTS:

A book was written about this house, which was later made into the a movie, Amityville Horror. This movie became the first of ten films made about this haunted dwelling.

This is one of the most controversial haunted houses in America.

Most of the paranormal encounters occurred during the time the Lutz family lived in the house in 1975. Terrified, they fled the house after living there just 28 days.

The History

Setting: Suffolk County, NY (Long Island)

Time: 6.35 P.M.

Date: November 13, 1974

The following is a transcript of a police call:

Operator: This is Suffolk County Police. May I help you?"
Man: "We have a shooting here. Uh, DeFeo."
Operator: "Sir, what is your name?"
Man: "Joey Yeswit."
Operator: "Can you spell that?"
Man: "Yeah. Y-E-S W I T."
Operator: "Y-E-S . .
Man: "Y-E-S-W-I-T."
Operator: ". . . W-I-T. Your phone number?"
Man: "I don't even know if it's here. There's, uh, I don't have a phone number here."
Operator: "Okay, where you calling from?"
Man: "It's in Amityville. Call up the Amityville Police, and it's right off, uh . . . Ocean Avenue in Amityville."
Operator: "Austin?"
Man: "Ocean Avenue. What the ... ?"
Operator: "Ocean ... Avenue? Offa where?"
Man: "It's right off Merrick Road. Ocean Avenue."
Operator: "Merrick Road. What's ... what's the problem, Sir?"
Man: "It's a shooting!"
Operator: "There's a shooting. Anybody hurt?"
Man: "Hah?"
Operator: "Anybody hurt?"
Man: "Yeah, it's uh, uh — everybody's dead."
Operator: "Whattaya mean, everybody's dead?"
Man: "I don't know what happened. Kid come running

in the bar. He says everybody in the family was killed, and we came down here."

Operator: "Hold on a second, Sir."

(*Police Officer now takes over call*)

Police Officer: "Hello."

Man: "Hello."

Police Officer: "What's your name?"

Man: "My name is Joe Yeswit."

Police Officer: "George Edwards?"

Man: "Joe Yeswit."

Police Officer: "How do you spell it?"

Man: "What? I just ... How *many* times do I have to tell you? Y-E-S-W-I-T."

Police Officer: "Where're you at?"

Man: "I'm on Ocean Avenue.

Police Officer: "What number?"

Man: "I don't have a number here. There's no number on the phone. "

Police Officer: "What number on the house?"

Man: "I don't even know that."

Police Officer: "Where're you at? Ocean Avenue and what?"

Man: "In Amityville. Call up the Amityville Police and have someone come down here. They know the family."

Police Officer: "Amityville."

Man: "Yeah, Amityville."

Police Officer: "Okay. Now, tell me what's wrong."

Man: "I don't know. Guy come running in the bar. Guy come running in the bar and said there — his mother and father are shot. We ran down to his house and everybody in the house is shot. I don't know how long, you know. So, uh . . ."

Police Officer: "Uh, what's the add ... what's the address of the house?"

Man: "Uh, hold on. Let me go look up the number. All right. Hold on. One-twelve Ocean Avenue, Amityville."

Police Officer: "Is that Amityville or North Amityville?"

Man: "Amityville. Right on ... south of Merrick Road."

Police Officer: "Is it right in the village limits?"

Man: "It's in the village limits, yeah."

Police Officer: "Eh, okay, what's your phone number?"

Man: "I don't even have one. There's no number on the phone. "

Police Officer: "All right, where're you calling from? Public phone?"

Man: "No, I'm calling right from the house, because I don't see a number on the phone."

Police Officer: "You're at the house itself?"

Man: "Yeah."

Police Officer: "How *many* bodies are there?"

Man: "I think, uh, I don't know — uh, I think they said four."

Police Officer: "There's four?"

Man: "Yeah."

Police Officer: "All right, you stay right there at the house, and I'll call the Amityville Village P.D., and they'll come down."

This story begins on November 13, 1974 when twenty-three-year-old Ron DeFeo murdered his entire family. Armed with a .35 Martin rifle, he crept into the bedrooms of his two sisters, two brothers, and parents and killed them as they lay sleeping.

Ron DeFeo claimed to be possessed by an evil spirit as his reason for the cold-blooded assassinations. This could be the beginning of the "Amityville Horror," if you believe DeFeo and others who claim there is something abundantly evil inside this dwelling. Defense attorneys also alleged that Ron's father had been abusive towards his son.

The prosecution argued that DeFeo had not been abused nor was he mentally ill. They told the jurors what they believed happened. Ron often argued with his father. Witnesses attested to that fact. They believed that on this particular night, Ron lashed out and killed his father either on purpose or in a fit of rage following a nasty argument. And with his adrenaline in overdrive, he got so carried away that he killed the rest of his family.

Ron DeFeo was found guilty. He was declared competent and fully responsible for the events of that night. He was sentenced to twenty-five years to life in prison.

Thirteen months later, along came the George and Kathy Lutz. They bought the 4,000-square-foot property in December 1975 for just $80,000. They even bought some of the DeFeo furniture for an additional sum. George and Kathy felt the large home would be the perfect place for their newly blended family. The lovely Dutch colonial sat on a picturesque canal. The large home featured a pool and boathouse.

Knowing the dark history of the house, George and Kathy arranged for a priest to bless the house. Father Ralph Pecoraro came to Amityville on December 18, 1975. (He was called Father Mancuso in the book to protect his identity). He had just taken the holy water out of his pocket when a disembodied voice demanded he "get out." He did not report the encounter to the Lutzes because he did not want to upset them. Instead, he continued with the blessing ritual. When he had finished, the couple thanked him and he promptly left. They finished unpacking and settling into their new home. Meanwhile, Father Pecoraro developed stigmata on his hands and a raging fever.

Exactly twenty-eight days later, the Lutzes

abandoned their new home. The family of five left almost everything behind when they fled the premises. George never made a single payment on the $60,000 mortgage. They defaulted to the lender on August 30, 1976. The family proclaimed the house "haunted" and refused to live there.

Instead, George and Kathy collaborated with Author Jay Anson to write *Amityville Horror*. The book became a best seller and was made into a series of blockbuster movies. Some feel the Lutz family made up the story to bail themselves out of a financial crisis. Others believe every word of this haunted tale.

That doesn't include the Cromarty family, who lived in Amityville after the Lutzes abrupt exodus. They paid $55,000 for the property in March 1977. They became terribly upset about the notoriety of the house and what had been reported as "true accounts." The Cromartys held a press conference to set the record straight. The following is an excerpt from the statement they read:

"The quiet village of Amityville, Long Island, has been made infamous by a hoax. It will possibly never be the same. It is Long Island's equivalent to Watergate. None of us would be here today if a responsible publisher and author had not given credibility to two liars, and allowed them the privilege of putting the word true on a book in which all actuality is a novel. The credibility of the hoax stems from using a charlatan Catholic priest, who has been banned from performing his religious duties by the Diocese of Rockville Centre, the

equivalent of disbarment of a lawyer. This charlatan priest has been involved with complicity to a lie, and, therefore, deserves no credibility, and should be dealt with accordingly."

The family went even further, suing the Lutzes, Jay Anson, and the book publisher. The parties reached an out-of-court settlement that was not made public. In an ironic twist, the Lutzes sued several parties: Ron DeFeo's defense attorney William Weber, freelance writer Paul Hoffman, Clairvoyants Frederick Mars and Bernard Burton, *Good Housekeeping, NY Sunday News,* and Hearst Corporation. George and Kathy sued for invasion of privacy, misappropriation of names for trade purposes, and mental distress. They sought nearly $5 million in damages. Countersuits were filed. All the suits were ultimately dismissed.

George and Kathy took lie detector tests, which they both passed. However, George admits that some things that have been reported are not true. But he adamantly denies there was any hoax or fraud involved.

The Lutzes met Jay Anson but never worked with him on the book, despite contrary accounts. Instead, they submitted almost 50 hours of audio cassettes to him, detailing their experiences. These recordings are what Anson referred to when writing the book, which was published in September 1977.

The Cromartys sold the house after living there for nearly ten years. They swear that nothing weird happened while they lived there. Amityville was purchased by Peter and Jeanne O'Neil on August 17,

1987. They lived there for a few years and made some renovations before selling it. It was sold to Brian Wilson on June 10, 1997. Wilson paid $310,000 for the estate. None of these owners has reported any paranormal encounters.

 The Hauntings

Is this house haunted or is it all a hoax? It depends on who you ask. This remains the most controversial haunted house in America.

What are some of the claims that Lutzes made?

*No matter how tired he was, George Lutz woke up every night at 3 a.m. and found himself compelled to go to the boathouse. He later learned that was the time Ron DeFeo began his killing spree.

*There were cold spots in random places in the house where it made no sense.

*The smell of perfume was prevalent in certain areas of the house for no good reason.

*George heard noises, such as a band playing and the front door slamming, that no other family member heard.

*Kathy swore that she was levitated two feet into the air while in bed. She also said that she was sometimes "touched" or "hugged" by unseen presence.

*Windows and door locks were regularly found to be damaged but they couldn't figure out how or by whom.

*They suffered swarms of flies even though it was middle of winter.

*The dog refused to go near a secret room they found in the basement.

George and Kathy held their own blessing ceremony on January 8, 1976 after all these strange events transpired. They claim that during the Lord's

Prayer, several voices commanded them to stop.

On January 14, 1976, the family left and never returned to Amityville. They had a mover box everything up and send their belongings to them.

Kathy and George divorced in the late 1980s. Kathy died on August 17, 2004 of emphysema. George died twenty-two months later of heart disease.

Some researchers have debunked the claims made by Kathy and George while others have validated them. Dr. Stephen Kaplan was one of many to investigate the haunting. The ghost hunter was called in by the Lutzes but had a falling out with George and Kathy at some point during the investigation. He went on to write a scathing book, *The Amityville Horror Conspiracy,* which was published in 1995.

However, several sources do back up the Lutzes' stories. One such source is Ed Warren. He is a demonologist who spent the night inside the house on March 6, 1976. He came with a reporter from WNEW-FM, Michael Linder, and a crew from Channel 5 TV in New York. They took time-lapse images that revealed "a demonic boy with glowing eyes standing at the foot of the staircase." This photograph was released to the public three years later. In 1979, the professional photographer and Lutz family appeared on the Merv Griffin Show, which was a popular talk show at that time. The famous photo was taken during the night by a camera placed on the second floor. It was set to automatically take photos throughout the night. Almost every photograph turned out completely black, except for one. This is the image of the little boy peering through the railing on the second floor. It is clearly a little boy, not an orb or shadowy figure. The question is, is the photo authentic? No one has been able to say definitively if it is real or faked, so the controversy continues.

Famous ghost investigator, Hans Holzer, conducted a paranormal investigation. He concurred with Ed Warren's assessment that the house is home to evil spirits. Some believe that George Lutz may have been a catalyst or conduit for the poltergeist. That may explain why no other homeowners reported any strange happenings. Perhaps it began and ended with George Lutz? Or could it simply be a hoax?

Visitor Information

112 Ocean Avenue

Long Island, NY 11701

Long Island is less than ten miles from Brooklyn, Jersey City (NJ), and New York City. The house can be found on the south end of the island.

The house is not open to the public. It is privately owned and visitors will not be permitted any closer than public streets or sidewalks. That is, if you can find the house. The property looks very different than it once did, thanks to renovations deliberately designed to throw off curious visitors. If you go there and stop to ask a local for directions or any other information related to Amityville, don't be surprised to receive an unfriendly response. Residents do not like the negative attention this story has spawned. They are very reluctant to talk about it to anyone outside the community.

The house came under new ownership in August 2010. It was sold for close to $1 million, which was close to the asking price. So far, the new owners have not come forth with any horror stories. But they must be less mindful of the attention their home draws because they have put an identifier plaque in front of the infamous edifice.

www.amityvillehorror.com

There have been ten Amityville Horror movies made:

- *The Amityville Horror* (1979) Starred James Brolin and Margot Kidder.
- *Amityville II: The Possession* (1982)
- *Amityville 3-D* (1983) (also released as *Amityville III: The Demon*)

- *Amityville 4: The Evil Escapes* (1989)
- *The Amityville Curse* (1990)
- *Amityville: It's About Time* (1992)
- *Amityville: A New Generation* (1993)
- *Amityville Dollhouse* (1996)
- *The Amityville Horror* (2005 remake)
- *The Amityville Haunting* (2011)

Price-Gause House

Price-Gause House

FUN FACTS:

The structure is included on a local ghost walk and participants sometimes claim they become nauseas and dizzy while at this property.

The house was built where executions were once performed and bodies were buried on the same grounds in unmarked graves.

The resident ghost "George" seems fond of cigars and sweet potatoes.

The History

During the mid-1700s to late 1800s, Wilmington was one of the biggest ports in North Carolina—and remains so to this day. Thanks to lumber production, shipbuilding, and the cotton exchange, people flocked to the bustling port city to find work and take up residence. In fact, the seaport had one of the biggest cotton exchanges in the world and was a leading producer of tar, pitch, and turpentine.

The house was built circa 1855-1860, although some sources say it was built in 1843. This isn't possible given that records prove that the original owner didn't buy the lot until 1854. The Italianate-style, three-story house was built by Lt. Colonel William Jones Price. He was a Wilmington doctor who later served in the Confederate Army. As soon as the family moved in, the haunting began.

The Cape Fear River brought with it a bad element, as well as commerce. Rowdy sailors arrived in port after being at sea for extended periods of time, thieves, ruffians, and other unsavory sorts arrived by ship and railroad. Many were found guilty of breaking the law and hanged on the very land where Price built his house.

The Hauntings

The problem is most likely the location, not the house itself. The residence was built on a burial site, which was once known as Gallows Hill. Presumably, Price didn't know this was a burial site or he would probably would have built elsewhere.

The 500 block of Market Street is where all the executions once took place in Wilmington. The executions drew large crowds. The public liked to see the criminal get what was coming to him and hear their final words. One of the many who were executed here was James Peckham. He was sentenced to death for stealing a purse. He swore his innocence right up until the noose was tied around his neck. Most of the folks who were executed had no family in town or none who would claim them. They were buried where they were executed—in unmarked graves.

This was confirmed in the 1970s. The owner was having work done on his home when contractors discovered tombs and human bones. The owner promptly told the contractors to rebury the tombs and bones.

It wasn't long after the Price family moved into their new home that the paranormal activity began. They usually occurred in the evenings when the family was gathered in the front parlor. They didn't see anything unusual but they heard all kinds of sounds: thumps, thuds, and footsteps overhead. Since they were all accounted for, this was a little frightening, at least in the beginning. After a while, they stopped going to investigate or giving it much thought.

Sometimes, the ghost moved objects and opened and closed doors. A rocking chair moved on its own on occasion. Beds were found messed up after servants swore they had made them. Servants also complained that they found dishes and silverware and items on the counter and in the sink after they had cleaned the kitchen. The children were immediately suspected even though they denied any involvement. However, they were soon ruled out because there were times they were not even home when this happened. Also, the cabinets where items had been removed were too high for the children to reach.

Tapping sounds were heard from within the walls from time to time. This disturbed the family more than anything else. They discussed these events with friends and neighbors. Reports of the house being haunted became wide spread. *Wilmington Star News* sent a reporter and photographer to the house. After a two-day stakeout that began on October 29, 1967, the men found nothing unusual. They were about to leave when they heard footsteps overhead. The only other person in the house at that time was the mother and she was in the kitchen. The men ran upstairs. They didn't find anyone but they found a rocking chair in one of the bedrooms that was still in motion, as if someone had just been in it.

While they were discussing this, they became aware of an unusual noise. They later described it as a "swishing sound." The two men saw something when they reached the hall, but were afraid their eyes were playing tricks on them. The photographer took several pictures and they hurried back to the newspaper to develop them. One of the pictures showed something clearly visible on film. It appeared as a human shape but was definitely not human. Some say this is a hoax, faked by the newspaper men and a family member.

That has never been proven or disproven. But even if this incident is not legitimate, there are lots of other unexplainable events that point to paranormal activity.

Although the house stayed in the Price family until 1968, they didn't live in it for several years prior to that. It was rented out and then bought by the Greater Wilmington Chamber of Commerce. They inhabited the building until 1990. Over the many years they owned the property, numerous employees reported odd experiences. One of the most common was the smell of pipe smoke and sweet potatoes baking when no one was baking or smoking. Lights and faucets turned on and off by themselves. So did electric typewriters. Maybe you can chalk those things up to electrical malfunctions or anomalies, but what about the figure that has been seen?

An old man wearing period clothing has been seen at the front door and on the front stairs, but disappears if anyone approaches. This figure has been called "George" ever since the director of the chamber hired a psychic to get to the bottom of all the strange goings on. The psychic offered a disturbing description and named the resident ghost, "George."

Several groups have investigated the property over the years, including Eastern Paranormal Investigations. The group picked up lots of interesting EVPs, as well as photo and video peculiarities. A team member claims to have "seen and spoken to a woman in period attire." J & J Ghost Seekers swear they witnessed a woman in an upstairs window peeking out from behind the curtains when no one was in the house.

Some visitors are adamant that they sensed an unseen presence inside the house. Sometimes, participants of a local ghost walk say they have experienced intense, sudden pressure and/or a funny feeling while they are standing in the side yard listening to the guide. This is reportedly where the executions took place.

The Price house is now home to an architectural firm. Its employees still hear footsteps and the strong smell of a pipe being smoked and sweet potatoes baking on occasion.

Visitor Information

The property is privately owned by a local business. However, it can clearly be seen from the street without trespassing and is included as a stop on a local ghost walk.

514 Market Street

Wilmington, NC 28401

Wilmington is 3.5 hours from Greensboro, NC (212 miles); 11 hours from Louisville, KY (675 miles); and 11.5 hours from Cleveland, OH (700 miles).

Octagon House

Octagon House

FUN FACTS:

The structure is actually hexagonal, not octagonal.

It was used as a temporary office and residence for President James Madison and briefly as a French Embassy.

The place is reportedly haunted by a half dozen ghosts.

The History

It was designed by the same architect who created the U.S. Capitol, which was Dr. William Thornton. It took two years to complete Colonel John Tayloe's second home (1798 – 1800). His primary residence was Mt. Airy Plantation, which was roughly 100 miles away in the neighboring state of Virginia. Tayloe was the richest plantation owner in Virginia at that time. Some argue that he was the richest in America or at least among the wealthiest.

It was reportedly built in this unusual shape because of the odd-shaped lot. Despite its name, the structure is actually hexagonal, not octagonal. While all the construction materials were manufactured locally, most of the decorative components and furnishings were imported from England.

There is no doubt that Tayloe needed the large

three-story brick house given that the couple had fifteen children. Mrs. Tayloe gave birth to eight girls and seven boys over the course of two decades.

The Tayloes offered the use of their home to President James Madison and his wife, Dolley, after the British set fire to the White House during the War of 1812. Many buildings throughout Washington were destroyed by the British during this time. The Octagon House was spared due to quick thinking on John Tayloe's part. He granted the French the right to use it as an embassy. With their flag flying over the house, the British didn't dare destroy it. During the time the President resided here, he used the upstairs parlor as his study. It was here that the Treaty of Ghent was signed on February 17, 1815. This resulted in a peace accord with Great Britain.

The Tayloes eventually sold their Washington, D.C. home in 1855. It was used as apartments for a while and then became home to the American Institute of Architects on January 1, 1899, although the sale was not finalized until 1902. It was a perfect fit with AIA given its architectural ingenuity. The design incorporated a circle, triangle, and two rectangles in a clever fashion. Architects also marvel at the use of Coade stone, Aquia Creek sandstone, ironworks, brickwork, and timber.

(Vestibule of Octagon House)

The Hauntings

Where to begin? Ladies first...

Colonel Tayloe's oldest daughter, Anne, was beautiful and rebellious. According to reports, Tayloe was blessed (or cursed?) with all of his daughters being very beautiful. Anne was one of the loveliest and most rebellious of his eight girls. Despite her father's hatred for the British, Anne began secretly dating a British soldier. The father discovered what Anne had been up to and forbade her from ever seeing the soldier again. The father and daughter got into a huge fight after he caught her sneaking into the house one evening. During this argument, Anne fell to her death. While some believed John pushed her during a fit of anger, it is more likely that she lost her balance and accidentally fell to her death.

Ever since that time, the ghost of Anne Tayloe is sometimes seen on the staircase. A more common occurrence is a light that looks like a candle being carried by an invisible source up and down the stairs. Some believe this is the reason John Tayloe sold the house. He got rid of it because he could no longer stand being haunted by the spirit of his deceased daughter.

Remarkably, John had another daughter who also fell to her death. It was also during an altercation with her father that it occurred. She ran away with a young man whom her father disapproved of. The relationship didn't work out and the girl came home. Her father did not welcome her with open arms. Instead, he chastised her for her rebellious behavior. Harsh words were spoken by both the daughter and father. Somehow, she stumbled backwards over the railing to her death. But some feel this was no accident. They think that John pushed his daughter in a moment of fury. A cold spot is often felt at the exact spot where her body landed, which was near the bottom of the stairs.

This grand oval staircase where both girls died is the centerpiece of the house. It is also where screams, thuds, and unexplained footsteps have been heard throughout the years. While some refute that these deaths happened here (some say the two daughters died at Mt. Airy), the strange encounters that many have witnessed over the years cannot be disputed.

The ghost of Dolley Madison may be here too. The first lady loved the smell of lilacs. She wore lilac perfume and kept vases of lilac flowers throughout the residence. Visitors have smelled lilacs when there are no such flowers present or anyone wearing any lilac-scented perfume or powder.

Former First Lady
Dolley Madison

Dolley often wore fancy turbans. She felt they added elegance and stature to her appearance. She came to be known for her sophisticated, feathered turbans. A shadowy figure wearing something on its head has been seen in the downstairs reception room, which is believed to be the spirit of Dolley. The sounds of glasses clinking and laughter in the dining room are attributed to Dolley, who loved to entertain. The open doors and blazing lights the caretakers often find in the dining room even after they have locked the doors and extinguished all lights are attributed to Dolley too.

Perhaps the strangest thing that has happened at the Octagon House is the bells. The bells that once summoned servants to various parts of the house were disconnected. This was done because the bells kept ringing when no one was ringing them—or at least no one admitted it and no one was found to be responsible. Nonetheless, they continued to ring regularly but when someone went to investigate the source, they never found anyone.

Even after the Tayloes moved out in 1855, the story doesn't end. A doctor made a house call during the 1950s. On his way upstairs to tend to the patient, he passed a man in a military uniform. He nodded and kept going. He found the attire curious and said as much to the caretaker. The man had no explanation for what the physician saw on the staircase. Some think this might be the British soldier looking for Anne. Others think it could be the spirit of James Madison looking for

Dolley.

Even the biggest skeptics cannot deny that something strange is going on here. Too many unexplainable events have been reported by visitors, caretakers, curators, other employees to ignore.

Visitor Information

The property is a National Historic Landmark and on the National Register of Historic Places. AIA still owns the building but has moved its offices to an outer building. The former residence has been converted into a museum. Tours can be arranged and there is a small admission fee. The property is located in the Foggy

Bottom neighborhood, just one block from the White House.

1799 New York Avenue (18th Street & New York Ave NW)

Washington, DC 20006

Washington, DC is one hour from Baltimore, MD (44 miles); 2 hours from Richmond, VA (110 miles); and 4.5 hours from Raleigh, NC (275 miles).

www.aia.org

Sorrel-Weed House

Sorrel-Weed House

FUN FACTS:

The structure is one of the most haunted buildings in Savannah, which is saying a lot given that Savannah is one of the most haunted cities in America.

It is considered to be one of the most important architectural buildings in Savannah; designed by renowned architect Charles Cluskey and has been designated a state landmark.

Lots of significant events have occurred here. Some scenes from the movie, Forest Gump, starring Tom Hanks, were filmed here. General Robert E. Lee attended a couple of parties held here. The Historic

Savannah Foundation held their first meeting here in 1939 (formerly called Preservation of Savannah Landmarks). It became a state landmark in 1954.

The History

This mansion brilliantly combines classic Greek Revival and Regency architectural styles. Construction began in 1835, but it was nearly five years before it was completed. It was the first residence built on Madison Square, which was considered one of the best addresses in the entire city. Francis could afford it given he was a wealthy shipping merchant.

Francis and Matilda Sorrel often threw lavish parties that often lasted until the wee hours of the morning. Even when there was not a party going on, the house was full of cheerful noise. This was due, in large part, to the eight children the couple had. (One of his sons went on to become one of the youngest generals in the Confederate Army). Between their many friends coming over to play and the large dinner parties thrown by Matilda, the house was always a happy, bustling place.

This ended abruptly one afternoon in May 1860. This was the day that Matilda caught her husband in bed with one of their servants. Legend has it that Matilda went looking for a missing servant named Molly. After knocking on the girl's bedroom door, she entered without waiting for an answer. She found her missing servant—and her husband—in bed together.

Matilda screamed in horror as she ran from the

room. Francis hurriedly threw on his clothes so that he could catch up with his wife. No telling how he planned to explain this "encounter" because he never got the chance. Matilda raced to the master bedroom where she pushed open the balcony door. Without hesitation, she flung herself over the balcony, plummeting to her death.

Francis arrived at the balcony too late to save his poor wife. This time it was he who screamed in horror as he watched her plummet to her death. He ran outside and cradled his dead wife in his arms, sobbing over what had transpired. He never got over the guilt of her death. He was so ashamed of himself that he was never the same again. Neither was the pretty, young servant girl.

She was found dead a few days later. Some believe he murdered her out of shame or to make sure that no one else learned of their dalliance. Others believe that she hanged herself, unable to accept her part in the tragedy. Francis Sorrel never talked about what had happened. He never remarried. And he never hosted another party.

 The Hauntings

Both Molly and Matilda haunt this property. Occupants are awakened on occasion by the sounds of music and laughter and muffled voices. Objects are sometimes moved from where the owners put them to where the ghosts think they belong. There is a huge, old cracked mirror in the hall and a blurry face is sometimes seen in it. Photographs that have been taken by amateur ghost hunters show orbs and ghostly handprints on the walls. SyFy's 'Ghost Hunters' conducted an investigation a few years ago and gave a rare pronouncement of "haunted." They even captured an EVP recording of a woman screaming, *"Get out. Help me. My God."*

A shadowy figure wearing a black dress with hoop skirt, an elaborate hat, and dark cape has been seen in the carriage house and in the courtyard. She disappears as soon as anyone tries to approach her. Some believe this is Matilda.

(Entrance to haunted courtyard)

Visitor Information

For those interested in finding out for themselves, there are a couple of options. There is a daytime historic tour and nightly ghost tours that includes use of EMF detectors and access to the most haunted areas of the property. There is information on their website about nightly ghost tours that include admission to the house, including the basement, carriage house, and voodoo room. All are considered to be among the most haunted places in the house.

6 W. Harris Street

Savannah, GA 31410

Savannah is 2 hours from Charleston, SC (112 miles); 2.5 hours from Augusta, GA (125 miles); and 4 hours from Charlotte, NC (250 miles).

www.sorrelweedhouse.com

Korner's Folly House

Korner's Folly House

FUN FACTS:

The structure has been dubbed "The Strangest House in the World."

The house has been officially certified as "haunted" by as many as four ghosts.

The first private theater in America was inside this house. The theater, Cupid's Park, still exists.

The History

The Strangest House in the World. That's what it was once called by an architectural magazine, *Preservation*, and the name stuck. It's no wonder it's considered such a strange dwelling. It is a three-story house that has seven levels. The 6,000-square foot Victorian mansion has twenty-two rooms with ceiling heights ranging from six feet to twenty-five feet. There are many unusual murals and artwork in the house, as well as a unique air distribution system. Another unusual feature is the smoking room. Accidental fires posed a serious threat in those days. With that in mind, a fireproof room was built onto the house. This is the only place that smoking was permitted within the house. No two doorways are the same. The same is true for the fifteen fireplaces. There are numerous cubbyholes and trapdoors throughout the odd house.

  The house was the architectural vision of one man, Jule Gilmer Korner. He began building the house in 1878. Two years later, he moved in but continued to make changes to the house for many years. It was built to showcase his interior design business, but later it became a home for his family.

  He hired a freed slave to run his household. She affectionately became known as 'Aunt Dealy.' She took good care of the house and Jule until he got married in 1886. After that, the job fell to his new wife, Polly Alice Masten Korner. A cottage was built behind the house and Aunt Dealy moved out of the main house and into this outbuilding.

Jule and Polly had two children. Child-sized rooms were constructed to accommodate them. Many other changes were made, such as the additions of a ladies sitting room and a library. The top story of the house was made into a children's theatre, Cupid's Park. Puppet shows, plays, and recitals were held here for all the children in town to enjoy. Theatrical productions are still produced here on occasion. Underneath the theatre is a huge room that is known as the Reception Room. This is where Jule and Polly did most of their entertaining.

Cupid's Park Theatre (top floor of house)

Because of its odd design and never-ending renovations, a visiting cousin once remarked that "This will surely be Jule Korner's folly." Instead of being offended, Jule was amused. He promptly had a plaque made that read "Korner's Folly" and hung it outside the front door.

Jule Korner died in 1924. Right up to his death he was still working on the house because he never felt that it was finished. Polly died ten years later. The property stayed in the family until the 1970s when it was turned over to the non-profit group, Korner's Folly Foundation.

The Hauntings

Korner's Folly has been investigated by several ghost groups and certified as officially haunted. I have spent the night inside the house, along with an investigative team from the Winston-Salem Paranormal Society. We hunkered down for the night in various rooms across the house, which were reportedly the most haunted areas. These included the Reception Room, Cupid's Park, the ladies sitting room, and one of the bedrooms.

The most haunted area of the house is believed to be the Reception Room, so this is where I chose to be. The psychic and a lead investigator were also in the room with me. The bulk of the monitoring equipment was set up here, so we could see what was going on in other parts of the house. The director of the foundation, Bruce Frankel, had given us a private tour and implicit instructions regarding our overnight stay. One of the rules was not to touch the furniture, so the three of us were seated in folding chairs in the middle of the room. Beside me was the "kissing couch." It has an "S" shape so that the man and woman can sit on opposite sides and face one another to talk or steal a kiss.

At one point in the evening, I suddenly felt very cold and got a weird sensation. As I was trying to figure this out given that it was a hot June night, I felt something on my arm. Startled, I soon realized that it was the hand of the psychic, who was seated next to me. He spoke softly, "I thought you should know that I sense a female presence on the kissing couch." I quickly processed what he was saying. A ghost was beside me!

She moved around the room, standing next to the piano and near the doorway before she disappeared. I knew when she had moved away from me because the cold (and weird) feeling disappeared as suddenly as it had occurred.

We had some questionable EVPs and one of the team members felt a pinch on her behind when no one was standing near her. That was believed to be the spirit of Jule, who had a reputation as a "ladies man" before he got married. He has been known to pinch female visitors on the behind sometimes during their tours.

Another group, Southern Paranormal and Anomaly Research Society (SPARS), certified the house as being "officially haunted" at the conclusion of their investigation. They picked up lots of EVPs of moaning and "peek-a-boo," which was a favorite game of the Korner children. The group also saw unexplainable shadows and orbs on their images.

If all the reports are true, then Korner's Folly is haunted by several spirits. These include Jule Korner, his kids, and Aunt Dealy and/or Polly Korner.

(Wide angle view of the haunted ballroom and kissing
couch)

Visitor Information

The house is open to the public for daytime tours. Also,
special events are held throughout the year. The biggest
and best is its Holiday Open House. During December,
the house is decorated to the hilt, usually by
professional interior designers. Take it from me, the
house looks properly festive. Jule Korner would be
proud!

413 S. Main Street

Kernersville, NC 27284

Kernersville is 2.5 hours from Asheville, NC (155 miles); 7 hours from Columbus, OH (390 miles); and 10.5 hours from Memphis, TN (650 miles).

www.kornersfolly.org

Wolfe Manor

Wolfe Manor

FUN FACTS:

This structure has been a home, sanitarium, and may soon become a boutique hotel.

This place was once dubbed "The Black Hole of Clovis."

The police receive 911 calls from the house even though there is no working phone. The phone lines were disconnected years ago.

The History

Clovis started out as a freight stop on the San Joaquin Valley Railroad in 1891. Despite being the 'Gateway to the Sierras' [as in Sierra Nevada Mountains],' the small town never became as big or as well-known as neighboring communities, such as Fresno, San Francisco, and Los Angeles. In fact, the last census poll revealed that the population remains less than 100,000 and there is not much industry or commercial activity to speak of. But ghost hunters can tell you what it does have—one of the most haunted houses in America.

An Italian immigrant named Tony Andriotti built a spectacular 8,000-square-foot mansion in circa 1922. According to legend, he built the grandiose house as part of a bet with his brother-in-law to see who could build the best home. The family lost the home during the Great Depression when they reportedly were unable to pay the taxes owed on it. It set vacant for a while before being bought and converted into the Hazelwood Sanitarium in 1935. It was a hospice for terminally ill patients.

This was transformed into the Clovis Sanitarium in 1942, which was intended to treat mentally ill patients. Although intentions may have been good, conditions were not. Patients were subjected to over-crowded and under-staffed conditions. The maximum number of patients was supposed to be 100 – 150, but hundreds of patients were confined here at any given time.

Since the patient to staff ratio was 20:1, the staff was unable to adequately care for many patients. Because of neglect, many patients suffered and died. The neglect contributed to bedsores, malnourishment, and patients being restrained by chaining them to beds, showers, chairs, and toilets. Reportedly, the number of deaths extends into the thousands during the fifty years the facility was in operation. The place got a bad reputation and became known to locals as "The Black Hole of Clovis."

The sanitarium was finally closed down by authorities. Once again, it sat vacant for many years, until Todd Wolfe purchased the property in 1997. He renamed it Wolfe Manor. The hospital wing that had been added to the house in 1942 was demolished in 1997.

The Hauntings

Wolfe opened the place as a haunted attraction 'Scream If You Can', not realizing that special effects and props were not needed. Wolfe Manor was a real haunted house. Visitors and workmen have reported many strange things, such as disembodied voices, cold spots, shadowy figures, being touched or pushed by an unseen presence, light-headedness, and nausea. A female reporter had her hair pulled during a tour and one guy was taken to the hospital with minor injuries after being knocked down.

Lots of psychics and paranormal groups have investigated over the years and found enough evidence to officially declare the place haunted. EVPs pick up cries, moans, and heavy breathing. EMF detectors have spiked wildly. Their levels reach well beyond normal range, indicating something strange is going on. Usually, when something like this happens, it is due to an electricity source. Since no electricity has been hooked up in the house in a long time these occurrences strongly suggest paranormal activity.

It is believed to be haunted by an elderly woman named Mary, a young girl known as Emily, a ghost named George, and at least two angry entities that remain unknown. They could be one or both of the murder victims or suicide. There are two documented murders that took place here. One patient was strangled by another patient and another patient was hanged by a patient. An elderly patient took his own life by turning a fire extinguisher on himself.

The most paranormal activity has been reported in Mary's bedroom, the kitchen, and the basement. A black entity has been seen going into Mary's old bedroom. It disappears quickly into the bathroom. Emily has been seen in the kitchen. Two angry entities haunt the basement. This is where pushing and tugging and unexplainable noises occur.

The most interesting thing is the 911 calls and the alarm system. The police regularly receive 911 calls and security system alarms coming from this house. However, this is not possible because the phone lines have been disconnected and there was never an alarm system installed!

Visitor Information

The owner is converting the house on Clovis Avenue into a boutique hotel (as you can see by the current condition of the property, he has his work cut out for him). When completed, it will have thirty-seven guest rooms, including Mary's Room and George's Room. Currently, it is closed for safety reasons (but the status may change at any time so be sure to check the Wolfe Manor page on Facebook and www.wolfmanorhotel.com for updates. He also does periodic broadcasts and investigations that he posts there. A small fire broke out in August 2012, but there was only minimal damage done to the interior. It is believed to have been arson.

Clovis is 6 hours from La Jolla, CA (335 miles); 17.5 hours from Denver, CO (1,144 miles); and 12.5 hours from Salt Lake City, UH (810 miles).

LaLaurie House

LaLaurie House

FUN FACTS:

The structure has been a residence, boarding house, luxury apartments, school, furniture store, bar, and torture chamber.

It is haunted by the spirits of dozens of slaves who were abused and who died here.

The LaLaurie family moved into the house in 1832 and then disappeared a couple of years later—never to be seen again.

 Delphine LaLaurie

The History

No wonder this is considered one of the most haunted houses in greater New Orleans. Unspeakable things went on inside this innocuous-looking edifice. Be warned that this story contains graphic content.

This story centers on Marie Delphine LaLaurie. She was one of the earliest documented female serial killers. She was married three times. Her final marriage (as far as we know) was to Leonard Louis Nicholas LaLaurie on June 25, 1825.

In 1832, Dr. Louis LaLaurie and Delphine moved into this house. It was one of the finest mansions in the French Quarter, even if the exterior was rather plain. Despite its façade, it was a sprawling, three-story mansion complete with intricate iron work, grand Mahogany doors, and massive chandeliers.

Delphine had good taste and spared no expense decorating her house on Royal Street. Only the best silver, crystal, candelabras, china, and exquisite flower arrangements were used when entertaining. Guests were suitably impressed as they stood on the black and white marble in the vestibule. They admired fine carved woodwork as they walked across the plush Oriental rugs and past fine European antiques and accessories to consume the best wines and delicacies of that era.

They found Delphine LaLaurie a charming and delightful hostess, who was eager to please her guests. But her staff saw none of that side of Madame LaLaurie. She behaved like a monster with her servants. The slaves were chained and beaten and treated horribly. She even whipped the young slave children.

A neighbor once witnessed Madame LaLaurie chasing a 12-year-old slave girl, Leah, past an upstairs window. Supposedly, Delphine became enraged when the girl tugged too hard while brushing her hair. She went ballistic, accusing the child of deliberately hurting her. She told Leah to stay put and await her punishment. Knowing this meant a violent beating, the girl ran. She bolted down the hall but there was nowhere to go. Trapped, the terrified girl climbed out a window onto the roof. When the angry mistress of the house pursued the girl waving a hefty whip in her direction, the girl chose to jump to her death rather than endure another ghastly beating. The neighbor watched in horror as Delphine LaLaurie smilingly peered over the edge of the rooftop to see the crumpled body on the ground below.

After more reports from neighbors who had repeatedly heard screams of anguish and seen signs of abuse, the authorities were dispatched to investigate. When they found slaves were malnourished, had been mistreated by obvious injuries, and some had even disappeared, they removed all the slaves. The law prohibited abuse of slaves and clearly the LaLaurie family had disregarded this mandate. The nine men, women, and children were sold at auction.

Unfortunately, Madame LaLaurie arranged for relatives to buy her slaves on her behalf. To their horror, all the slaves were promptly returned to her. They were savagely dealt with for their confessions to the authorities.

But the word was widespread by now. All of New Orleans society had learned about how Madame LaLaurie treated her slaves. They were appalled and ashamed. She was ostracized by her peers. Her dinner invitations were politely and repeatedly declined and the family was no longer invited to any social functions.

It all came to an end for the LaLauries in April 10, 1834. A fire swept through the house. According to a story in the *New Orleans Bee*, it was started by an elderly slave cook who could take no more. The woman, who was chained by her ankle most of the time to the kitchen stove, started a fire that rapidly spread through the house. Remarkably, she survived the fire and shared her confession with the firefighters who saved her. While the firefighters were checking the house for other survivors, they found the most horrific scene—a torture chamber. Hidden behind a secret door in the attic, they found mutilated bodies and torture apparatus. Some were still wearing spiked iron collars and were shoved into cages.

Most were missing body parts and had obviously suffered despicable deaths. Reportedly, the sight was so gruesome that all the firefighters fled the house and refused to return. Doctors had to be called to carry away the disfigured bodies. It wasn't long before everyone in New Orleans had heard the news. Angry citizens of all classes gathered in the streets demanding justice. As they marched towards the house carrying ropes and lanterns, a carriage tore through the gates.

Presumably, the LaLaurie family was inside the carriage, making their escape. They were never seen again. Reports vary greatly as to what happened to the family. Some sources say Madame LaLaurie moved to Paris and died from a boar attack while on a hunting expedition. Others say the family was taken in by relatives in Louisiana or Alabama.

The Hauntings

While the LaLauries may never have been seen or heard from again, the same cannot be said for the ghosts at 1140 Royal Street. Every occupant has witnessed bizarre goings on. All have claimed to have heard moaning, chains rattling, screams, and tortured cries. Some have even seen dark figures in chains. Others have been chased by mutilated specters brandishing whips and paddles.

Some owners and renters have lasted only a few days, while others manage to stay a few months. It has sat vacant for prolonged periods of time before the next brave (or ignorant) soul moves in.

One such owner was Jules Vignie. He was a member of an affluent family. He was also considered to be rather eccentric. With all his wealth, he chose to sleep on a cot in a dirty, cluttered room of a derelict property. Upon his death in 1892, thousands of dollars was found hidden in his bedroom. Reports of large sums of money hidden throughout the house were rampant, yet few dared to go inside the creepy house to find it.

Capitalizing on its dark history, one man opened a bar aptly named 'Haunted Saloon'. He kept a journal of every paranormal event reported to him by his staff and patrons.

Later, the old house was transformed into a furniture store. The business didn't last for long. The owner kept discovering damaged furniture when he arrived to open the store. He thought hooligans were breaking in at night and partying, which explained the stains on the upholstery. Armed with a shotgun, the owner hid in a corner and waited for the party to begin. Tonight, the thugs would get more than they bargained for! After waiting for hours for something to happen, the man dozed off. When sunlight streamed in through the front windows, he yawned and stretched, slowly emerging from his hiding spot.

As he crossed the room, he was amazed to find fresh stains on the furniture. But he was certain that no one had broken into the building. He was awake most of the night, but even during the two or three hours he had dozed off, he would have been awakened if any activity had occurred. When he realized that something supernatural must be happening, he closed down the shop. It was one thing to tangle with vandals, but he wasn't about to take on malevolent spirits!

The grave of the slave girl, Leah, has been discovered in back of the house and bodies and body parts have been found hidden under a floor board. Presumably, ghosts linger at the old LaLaurie house hoping to avenge their gruesome deaths...

Visitor Information

1140 Royal Street (at the corner of Royal and Governor Nicholls Streets in the famed French Quarter)

New Orleans, LA 70116

New Orleans is one hour from Baton Rouge (70 miles); 3 hours from Pensacola, FL (200 miles); and 8 hours from Little Rock, AR (440 miles).

Actor Nicholas Cage bought the property in 2007 for $3.45 million. It was foreclosed on by the bank in 2009. It was auctioned off to Regions Financial Corporation for $2.3 million. It remains a private residence. The owners have not shared reports of paranormal activity, so the last haunted encounter is unknown. But with a place full of so much grim history, there is little doubt that spirits still linger here.

Note: Madame Marie LaLaurie should not be confused with Madame Marie Laveau. Laveau was a famous voodoo priestess. Her story is included in *A Ghost Hunter's Guide to The Most Haunted Places in America*. Laveau's residence wasn't far from the LaLaurie house, which made them neighbors.

Voodoo Priestess Marie Laveau was born on Santo Domingo, Dominican Republic (September 10, 1794 – June 16, 1881). The earliest records placing her in New Orleans was in 1819, when she married Jacques Paris. He died in 1826 and Marie soon met Christophe

Glapion. This is the father of her daughter, Marie. Marie II was one of fifteen children that Marie I had, but became her most famous offspring. Both women became well-known and sought after voodoo priestesses.

Prospect Place

Prospect Place

FUN FACTS:

Despite being built in 1856, the house had "air conditioning" and a refrigeration system.

The house, also known as Trinway Mansion, was designed and built to be an Underground Railroad Station.

The house was the site of death, suicide, and suffering. Many victims of a nearby train wreck were brought to the house, where some eventually succumbed to death.

The History

Prospect Place is a 9,500-square foot mansion with 29 rooms. The Greek Revival and Italianate style house was built by George Willison Adams in 1856. It is actually the second home built on this site. The first was destroyed by an arsonist soon after it was completed. Like his father, he was strongly opposed to slavery and grew up to be an abolitionist. He and his brother, Edward, went into business together. They opened a flouring mill, which became a stop on the Underground Railroad. It was so successful that they added another mill near Dresden.

Adams became very affluent. He was president of Indiana Railroad. In addition to the mill, he owned warehouses, a boat yard, and copper shops. He also owned a 15,000-acre plantation, Prospect Place.

George and Edward's flour mill enterprise involved shipping to and from New Orleans, Louisiana. They used their business to help escaped slaves. They picked up slaves in New Orleans and hid them below deck when they delivered flour by boat. They brought them to Dresden, Ohio where they would continue their journey to freedom.

The house was specially built to hide slaves. There was a watch room at the top of the house with windows on all sides. When it appeared to be safe, the slaves fled the sanctuary of the basement. If a lantern was lit in the window of the cupola that meant it was safe for slaves to be brought into the house. The basement had been built with fireplaces to keep the slaves warm and comfortable. There was a cistern in the basement so that bounty hunters and authorities could not monitor water levels and usage of a well. (If water usage was abnormally high for the number of registered occupants, they knew that slaves were being hidden on the property).

Like his father who had thirteen children, George had a large family which included ten children. He had four with his first wife, Clarissa, and six with the woman he married after Clarissa's death. George Willison Adams died on August 31, 1879. He was 79 years old. At the time of his death, his estate was worth $14 million. His wife received half of the estate. Mary Jan Robinson Adams survived her husband by more than thirty-five years.

The house has remained in the family. George Cox, the grandson of G.W. Adams, owned it until the 1960s. It was sold to a distant relative, Eugene Cox, in 1969. His family owned the property until the 1990s.

Neglect and vandalism took a toll on the historic property until 20001 when George J. Adams bought the place. It became the G.W. Adams Education Center in 2005. Restorations are ongoing. The property is on the National Register of Historic Places and on the Ohio Underground Railroad Association's list of Underground Railroad sites. It is the last mansion still in existence in this part of Ohio.

The Hauntings

The house is reportedly haunted by several spirits. In 1912, a train broke down on the tracks about four miles from the mansion. It was hit by another train. Some passengers were badly injured and brought to the mansion, where some may have died from their injuries. Some believe their spirits linger here.

George Adams died of meningitis in his bedroom. His spirit may still be here. Some believe that the spirit of his second wife, Mary, lingers at Prospect Place. William Cox married George's daughter, Anna. They moved into Prospect Place and renovated the old homestead. They had a son and lived a happy life until he mysteriously disappeared one day. It is widely believed that Cox couldn't deal with being bankrupt. Unable to cope, he simply got on a train to Columbus one morning and left. He checked into the Schrader's Hotel with another man who did not sign the registry and checked out the next day. He was never seen again.

Or was he? A former resident of Dresden claims she saw William Cox while walking down the street in San Francisco. She called his name and he disappeared into a shop. She followed him but he eluded her. She wrote to Anna to report the strange incident. That was the last Anna heard about her missing husband. She never pursued the lead.

Anna was left to manage as best she could with what money that was left and as a single parent. Eventually, she broke her hip and died of pneumonia a few weeks later. Some of the runaway slaves may have died of injuries and illness while hiding at the house. One reportedly had a head injury when she arrived and died in the basement, but that has not been proven. From the 1960 – 1980s, satanic rituals were performed in the vacant house by a local cult. They used the large ballroom for their sacrifices and rituals.

Visitors have been grabbed by an invisible force. Unexplained noises and footsteps have been heard. Disembodied hissing sounds have been heard and EVPs have picked up "get out!"

One of the bedrooms is known as the "Bad Room." A sick child wandered out onto the front portico balcony one night. She was burning up with fever and sought relief in the winter night's cold temperature. In her delirium, she stumbled and fell from the balcony to her death. Since the ground was too hard to dig, the corpse was kept in the basement until spring when the ground thawed enough to allow a burial. Since that time, the spirit of a little girl has been seen in the basement, second floor near where the portico balcony once was, and in the upstairs parlor, which was used as her bedroom at that time. In this former bedroom, a child's voice is sometimes heard, as as well as girlish laughter and whispering. A small shadow has been seen at the foot of the bed.

In the middle of the "Bad Room," a woman has been seen that is believed to the spirit of Anna Adams-Cox. A man in period clothing has been seen throughout the house and that is believed to be William Cox, who may still be seeking peace after abandoning his family more than a century ago. The spirit of a servant has been seen on the stairwell.

The most haunted place on the property is the Barn. The three-story brick horse barn and carriage house is actually the remains of the original house. The original house was burned down to the foundation by an arsonist. Using the remains, the structure you see today was built. The third floor was used as sleeping quarters for farm hands, the second floor was used for storage, and the main level was used as stables and for the carriage.

According to records, a bounty hunter came to Prospect Place in the 1850s. He demanded that G.W. Adams surrender any slaves he had hiding in his house. George Adams responded by brandishing his pistol and ordering the man to leave. Someone slipped out the back and ran to the barn and told the men what was going on. They grabbed their rifles and hurried to the house. Seeing the men that surrounded him, the bounty hunter quickly departed. According to legend, the farm hands decided the world would be a better place with one less bounty hunter. They located his camp, kidnapped the man, and brought him back to the plantation. They hanged him inside the barn and then buried the body. They never told the Adams family or anyone else what they had done. Many feel sure that the spirit in the barn is that of the executed bounty hunter.

Many visitors have been touched by it, but no one has been harmed yet. Some visitors claim to feel nauseas while inside the barn. Over the years, hundreds of unexplained events have transpired, including people hearing their name called when no one is there and a disembodied voice whispering "join us." A demonologist investigated some years ago and declared the barn was not haunted but that it was home to a demonic presence.

In another interesting aspect of this story, the arsonist who set the fire is believed to be a neighbor, a Native American Indian. According to legend, the elderly woman was angry that the house was built on what was a supposedly ancient burial ground for her people. If this is true, construction on top of graves could explain some of the hauntings. But this story has never been substantiated.

Visitor Information

12150 Main Street

Trinway, Ohio 43842 (12150 County Rd. 706)

Note: Trinway is a half-mile north of Dresden.

Trinway is 2.5 hours from Cleveland, OH and Pittsburgh, PA (122 miles); and 6.5 hours from Bethesda, MD (359 miles).

www.gwacenter.org and www.prospectplace-dresden.com

Weekend tours are given and seasonal events are held. Overnight ghost investigations can be arranged.

Sprague Mansion

Sprague Mansion

FUN FACTS:

After the structure was renovated by the historical society, ghostly sightings have increased.

Amasa was  *brutally murdered within sight of Sprague Mansion.*

The creepiest room in the house is the Doll Room.

The History

The first owner of this home was William Sprague, who made his fortune from his company, Cranston Print Works. The company made calico cotton cloth at reasonable prices. This had never been done before. This was a gamble for the Sprague family. They already had a small, but successful cotton mill. But they took a risk and invested a tidy sum in machinery. Being the first business in America to print calico, there was good opportunity for profits.

With William's business savvy, he found a way to keep production costs low and output high. The company grew exponentially. Then one night in 1836, William Sprague choked on a chicken bone during dinner and died. After his death, his two sons, Amasa and William Jr., took over the business. They changed the name to A & W Sprague Company.

While they were equal partners in the enterprise, Amasa ran it while William Jr. focused on this true passion—politics. And he was successful at it. He served as a U.S. Representative, Governor, and U.S. Senator. However, he was forced to leave politics and return home to take control of the family business when his brother was murdered. On December 31, 1843, Amasa Sprague left the Sprague mansion on a business trip. His body was found on New Year's Day not far from his house.

William was married to Kate Chase, who was the daughter of Secretary of Treasury, Salmon Chase. Salmon went on to become Chief Justice of the United States Supreme Court. William and Kate moved into the Sprague mansion after Amasa's untimely death.

But who killed him and why?

The finger soon pointed at one man. An Irish immigrant named John Gordon tried to open a pub near the A & W Sprague Company. This was not something that the Sprague family wanted to happen. With the pub set to open across the street from the factory, they feared that employees would be inclined to stop in for a "quick one" before their shifts and or consume a pint or two during their breaks. They were confident that the pub would negatively impact production.

Amasa used his clout to make sure that the liquor license was not granted to John Gordon. The Gordons found out what Amasa Sprague had done. This created a vendetta.

Many believe this vendetta was fulfilled when John Gordon murdered Amasa Sprague. There was a sham of a trial following the arrest of Gordon. Although there was no evidence, John Gordon was found guilty and hanged for the crime. After the execution, evidence was uncovered that exonerated John Gordon. This led to the law regarding capital punishment in Rhode Island being changed forever. Capital punishment was outlawed after an innocent man was executed. (Some accounts say William Sprague or Gordon's brother committed the crime, but the truth is that the killer was never caught).

By the Civil War, William Sprague was the richest man in America. Developing the first chemical bleaching process helped secure the family fortune. Remarkably, by the late 1800s, the Sprague family was broke. After the collapse of Sprague industries, the house was sold and converted into a boarding house. It was bought by the Cranston Historical Society in 1967.

The Hauntings

The house, dating back to 1790, is a classic New England home. Originally, it was a two-and-a-half-story structure with a gable roof. Additions to the residence were later made that doubled the size of the estate. The house has beautiful features, including an impressive staircase complete with mahogany railing and Italianate marble fireplaces. Additionally, a carriage house was built, along with fabulous formal gardens. Today, visitors can see furniture and furnishings from the

Rhode Island Historical Society's Carrington Collection.

Perhaps the magnificent manor and fine furniture are the reason the ghosts linger here? An apparition has been seen on the grand staircase. Some say that it starts to descend the stairs before disappearing and it is unclear whether it is a man or woman. An unseen presence has been reported by many in the wine cellar, as well as inexplicable cold spots.

An informal séance was held in 1968 by the caretaker. It revealed that one of the spirits is most likely a disgruntled butler named Charles.

The first documented activity goes back as far as the early 1900s. Some have reported seeing creepy reflections in the cupola. The most common complaints are unexplained footsteps, an apparition seen or sensed, and lights turning on and off by themselves in the Doll Room. Visitors often say they feel "creeped out" while in the Doll Room, but it may be more from all the dolls staring at them than a real entity.

Most believe that at least one of the spirits is Amasa Sprague, whose murder was never avenged. The ghost of Lucy Chase Sprague, who was William and Kate's daughter, haunts the place too. She made some bad investments and lost a significant part of the family fortune. Another spirit who some say haunts the property is William Sprague IV. He was so devastated by the collapse of the family fortune that he took his life inside the house in 1890.

Paranormal investigations have occurred here and while the groups agree that it is haunted, they cannot say for sure who haunts it.

Visitor Information

1351 Cranston Street

Cranston, RI 02920

Cranston is five miles southwest of Providence; 2 hours from Hartford, CT (85 miles); 8 hours from Ocean City, MD (410 miles); and 29 hours from Ft. Worth, TX (1,800 miles).

It is open to the public. Tours are given by the Cranston Historical Society and it can be rented out for special functions.

www.cranstonhistoricalsociety.org

Fun Quiz

1. Why did Sarah Winchester keeping building onto the Winchester House?
2. How many were found dead inside the Villisca house?
3. The most haunted area of Prospect Place is the front parlor. True or false?
4. Where is Loretta Lynn's haunted mansion located?
5. What has Korner's Folly come to be known as (hint: nickname)?
6. What is the name of the resident ghost in the Price-Gause House?
7. The Octagon House is the biggest eight-sided house in the U.S. True or false?
8. The Lutz family lived in Amityville house just 28 days before fleeing, never to return. True or false?
9. Whaley House has been officially declared haunted by the U.S. Commerce Department. True or false?
10. What did authorities find when they investigated the LaLaurie House after a servant deliberately set a fire?

Quiz Answers:

1. She thought she would die if construction ever ceased, so she had workman at the house 24/7—until she died; 2. (8) Both parents, four children, and two visiting neighbor girls; 3. False. The barn is the most haunted; 4. Hurricane Mills, TN; 5. Strangest House in the World (first dubbed so by architectural magazine, *Preservation*; 6. George; 7. False. Octagon House is actually hexagonal; 8. True; 9. True; 10. Secret torture chamber created by Delphone LaLaurie to torment slaves. Authorities found torture devices and mutilated bodies.

Titles by Terrance Zepke

Ghost Books:

A Ghost Hunter's Guide to The Most Haunted Houses in America (Safari Publishing)

A Ghost Hunter's Guide to The Most Haunted Places in America (Safari Publishing)

Lowcountry Voodoo: Tales, Spells and Boo Hags (Pineapple Press)

The Best Ghost Tales of South Carolina (Pineapple Press)

Ghosts of the Carolina Coasts (Pineapple Press)

Ghosts and Legends of the Carolina Coasts (Pineapple Press)

The Best Ghost Tales of North Carolina (Pineapple Press)

Ghosts of Savannah (Pineapple Press)

Ghosts of the Carolinas for Kids (Pineapple Press)

Travel Guidebooks:

The Encyclopedia of Cheap Travel: Save Up to 90% on Lodging, Flight, Tours, Cruises and More! (Lookout Publishing)

Coastal South Carolina: Welcome to the Lowcountry (Pineapple Press)

Lighthouses of the Carolinas (Pineapple Press)

Coastal North Carolina (Pineapple Press)

Other Titles:

Pirates of the Carolinas (Pineapple Press)

Pirates of the Carolinas for Kids (Pineapple Press)

Lighthouses of the Carolinas for Kids (Pineapple Press)

Index

A

B

C

K

L

M

Y

Turn the page for a special preview
of the first book in Terrance
Zepke's 'most haunted' series:

A GHOST HUNTER'S GUIDE TO THE MOST HAUNTED PLACES IN AMERICA

Available from Safari Publishing

Shanghai Tunnels

FUN FACTS:

Portland has many nicknames, such as "Shanghai Capital of the World," "Worst Port in the World," "City of Roses," "Forbidden City," and "Unheavenly City." Most are related to its history of shanghaiing.

Men could go out for a few drinks and wake up at sea if they drank at the wrong place! Women were also abducted and forced into prostitution.

The tunnels are open to the public and visitors can choose from a variety of tour options, such as the "Shanghai Tunnel Ethnic History Tour" and "Shanghai Tunnel Ghost Tour."

The History

Merchants dug a network of tunnels under the city to transport merchandise to the water because it was easier than using the muddy, crowded streets to get the items to waiting ships. The tunnels also became a perfect way to handle human trafficking or shanghaiing.

Shanghaiing was an illegal activity but one that was widespread. It happened in Oregon and all over the world. Part of the problem is that local authorities and law enforcement denied its existence, tending to pretend it was not a problem.

By the mid-1800s, maritime trade was booming and there were not enough men for the crews, especially due to the Gold Rush. Ships from all over came to town and spent money while "shopping" for sailors. Also, it cut down on the transient and undesirable population. And shanghaiing served to fill a real need so perhaps they thought they were doing their civic duty!

Captains were always short-handed and resorted to some disturbing practices to find able-bodied men. They hired men, known as "shanghaiiers" to help them get good men. This was accomplished going to waterfront taverns where there was lots of drinking and commotion. During the course of the night, men were plied with drinks and a good meal that might be doped with a sleep aid. When the men fell asleep or passed out, they were taken to holding cells.

Once the shanghaiiers were paid the fees, they turned the men over to the captains. They were then transported to waiting ships through a series of tunnels that extended across a city (and under key buildings and businesses) down to the waterfront.

For approximately one hundred years, shanghaiing happened in waterfront towns all over the world. Among the places with the highest incidents was Portland, Oregon. It is believed that more than 2,000 people were shanghaied here during 1850 – 1940. Some put the figure much higher. Regardless of the exact number, it is obvious why Portland has been nicknamed "The Shanghai Capital of the World."

Sailors, loggers, farmers, gypsies, ranchers, cowboys, pirates, transients, and any other healthy male who frequented establishments with tunnel access underneath, such as Snug Harbor Saloon, Valhalla Saloon, Lazlo's Saloon, and Erickson's Saloon were likely to wake up somewhere far away. Reportedly, it took two full voyages or six years, for these men to get back home to Portland. Most of the ships were headed far away—to Shanghai, China. This is how the practice came to be called "shanghaiing."

A remarkably sophisticated system of tunnels snaked their way across the city from the North End

(Old Town and Chinatown) to the South End (downtown). The tunnels, known now as the Portland Underground, were built under places that were likely to draw men, such as saloons, brothels, gambling parlors, and opium dens. Transients, such as cowboys, sheep herders, and migrant farmers were ideal victims. After they had been plied with so much alcohol as to be drunk enough not to put up a fight (or given knock out drops), they were lured away to well-placed trap doors.

Men waited in the tunnel under the trap door for the men and women to be dropped. They caught the drunk or drugged bodies and dragged them to holding cells to await their fate. Their shoes were taken to impede escape and broken glass was reportedly scattered through the tunnels in case they came to and managed to escape their holding cells. Just before a ship's departure, the victim was again given knock out drops and carried to the waiting vessel. By the time the victim woke up, he would be far away.

During archaeological digs, old shoes have been found in the tunnels, substantiating the stories about the removed shoes.

 The Hauntings

It's no wonder these 6' x 6' holding cells and tunnels are haunted what with so much misery and tragedy.

And it wasn't just men. Women were often abducted and forced into prostitution. If they refused, they were murdered. Men and women were drugged and carried out secret basement doors to the holding cells and tunnels. However, some never made it any farther. Some died as a result of the fall of being thrown or dropped through the secret trap doors.

One spirit that haunts these tunnels is believed to a woman who died when deposited into a holding cell. Today, the business is a pizzeria but back when it was a shanghai hotspot; Nina was hustling business one night when she was drugged and thrown down into the holding cell. She hit her head and suffered internal injuries that resulted in her death. Ever since that time, her spirit haunts this place. She has been seen, her perfume smelled, and she has been known to tug on the clothing of tour participants.

But Nina is not the only ghost in these tunnels. There are believed to be several spirits unhappily trapped here. Their presence is shown in many ways, such as faint whispers, moans, cries, strange lights and shapes that appear in photos, and the smell of alcohol and cologne.

Tour operators installed thirteen sets of wind chimes in the tunnels. They call them "spirit chimes." Whenever they swing or ring, that means the spirits are nearby because there is no air flow to trigger the chimes.

There were a few prostitution rooms in the tunnel. A sheet hung like a curtain covered a small bed. There were rooms above the saloon that were also used for prostitution, but those were 'willing participants'. The shanghaied women were kept in the tunnels or sold into slavery.

Ghost groups have detected paranormal activity using EVPs, thermal imaging, and shadow detectors, which show unexplainable light shadowy mist. Some visitors to the tunnels report feeling lightheaded, dizzy and/or queasy feeling. Unexplained footsteps are heard and the sounds of old doors "creaking" open.

Visitor Information

Tours are offered by the non-profit group, Cascade Geographic Society. They last ninety minutes and explain the history and haunting of these tunnels. I've seen some unfavorable reviews online by participants who say they saw only a small brick room or holding cell under a business. I believe they are mistaking this experience given by a local business with the full tour provided by Cascade Geographic Society.

The tour starts above ground at Hobo's Restaurant at 120 N.W. Third Avenue. Hobo's was formerly Lazlo's Saloon and one of several sites renowned for shanghaiing. The restaurant does not take reservations or give tours. For more information, visit www.cgsstore.tripod.com, www.shanghaitunnels.info

Portland is 3 hours (173 miles) from Seattle, Washington and 15 hours (962 miles) from Los Angeles, California.

CPSIA information can be obtained at www.ICGtesting.com
Printed in the USA
LVOW01s1615130214

373591LV00018B/853/P

9 780985 539832